CANVASES
OF COURAGE

MARLYSE TOVAE *Grasshopper* Mosaic

First published in England 1991 by
Leader Books Limited
Barford Court
Lampard Lane
Churt
Surrey

ISBN 0 907159 02 8

Cover picture: Arnulf Stegmann   *Italian Lakes*

Photographs taken specially for this book were by
the author and Simon Alexander

Printed in England by Arrowhead Printing Limited
Unit 3, Park Works, Kingsley, Bordon, Hampshire.

CANVASES
OF COURAGE

BY
MARC ALEXANDER

LEADER BOOKS

PAST MASTERS

Erich Stegmann

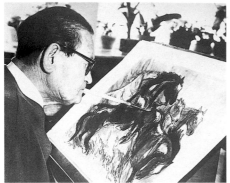

Carl Fischer

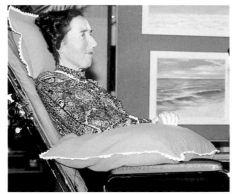

Elizabeth Twistington Higgins

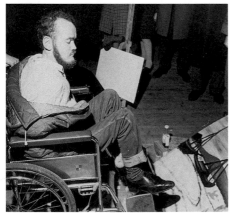

Christy Brown

Peter Spencer

Charles Fowler p97

Margaret Greig p99

Tom Yendell p181

Kris Kirk p103

Steven Chambers p68

Tommy Waru p176

James Claude Duncan p79

Alison Lapper p110

Florence Bunn p60

Joy Clarke p71

John Smith p146

John Butler p64

Mojgan Safa p137

Wendy Barber p49

John Bunce p57

Bruce Peardon p118

Heather Strudwick p149

Peter William Van Der Hulst p172

Derrick Vandek p169

Albert Baker p29

William W. Mooney p113

Paul Driver p76

Trevor Wells p178

Grant William Sharman p142

John Savage p139

Alexander Craig p74

Glenn Barnett p53

Erich Krell p107

INTRODUCTION

PAINT, BRUSH AND SPIRIT

*P*ede Pinxit — painted by foot — were the words that the Belgian artist Charles Felu used to sign his paintings. One of the great artists of the 19th century he was also regarded as a phenomenon because of his remarkable method of painting. Born without arms in 1830, he taught himself to paint with a brush held between his toes so skillfully that his work was eagerly collected by royalty and he was proud to number 'three kings and an emperor' among his friends.

Charles Felu, however, was only twenty when England's first recorded mouth painter died. In Somerset Sara Biffen had arrived in the world without limbs in 1784 and became so successful with a mouth-held paint brush that her work was hung in the Royal Academy.

Today the word 'phenomenon' is no longer applied to such artists — there are over three hundred men and women belonging to the Association of Mouth and Foot Painting Artists throughout the world.

The Association is the dream-come-true of the disabled German artist Arnulf Erich Stegmann whose story is included in these pages. It was his belief that if disabled painters with talent equal to that of able-bodied professional artists could form a partnership to have their work published, each could achieve personal independence regardless of the nature of his or her physical handicap.

To Erich Stegmann the key word was *partnership* — the word *charity* was abhorrent to him — and the Association has always been at pains to make it clear that it is not a charity and does not qualify for charitable assistance.

Ever since Erich Stegmann roamed the world in search of artists or potential artists who could benefit by joining the partnership, the Association has sought new members. The first step is for their work to be evaluated and if their standard is sufficiently promising they are invited to become students. As such they receive stipends to help them towards full membership with art materials, tuition and specially designed equipment if required. The latter may include such things as electric wheelchairs or vans adapted to carry wheelchairs which are beyond the reach of most disabled people living on welfare benefits.

An independent panel of art specialists frequently reviews the students' work and when one has reached a standard judged to be the equivalent to that of non-disabled professionals membership is granted. This means that the member will receive a monthly income for life regardless of whether increasing disability makes it impossible for him or her to continue providing pictures which the Association can market as greetings cards. This removes the greatest anxiety to haunt the handicapped artist — the fear of losing one's ability through deteriorating health, at the cost of

ERICH STEGMANN
Street Singers
Tempera   32 x 23 cm

ERICH STEGMANN
Regatta in Burano
Tempera

IWAO ADACHI
Castle in Bavaria
Oil   90 x 65 cm

9

independence for the disabled, is high. This is especially so for those who can only live on their own if they have regular helpers.

Several members told me that one of the best moments in their lives was writing to the Social Security authorities to announce that they no longer needed state aid as at last they were able to earn their own living. I have even heard of the pleasures of paying income tax!

The period of studentship varies a great deal and can be affected by the nature of the student's handicap. One of the advantages of the system is that it gives the student a goal to strive for — a purpose in life instead of what can so easily become a day-to-day existence with television as an anodyne.

Coming into contact with mouth and foot painting artists is always a fascinating experience for me because each is different in regard to age, background, faith and, of course, style of painting. And not only have I met the artists but in many cases their pets; indeed a book could be written about these ranging from John Chambers' chinchilla to Margaret Greig's miniature horse. If anyone should ever doubt the understanding of animals they should see those belonging to disabled artists. They *know* the situation and their companionship is unstinted for those who are unable to throw balls or stroke fur.

In this book we meet artists of Britain, Australia and New Zealand but it should be remembered that the Association has members in forty-seven countries including some behind the rusting Iron Curtain. Now that there have been such historical changes in Eastern Europe it is likely that more students will be enrolled there.

In order to not overlook this international aspect it was decided to include a token example of work by an artist outside the English-speaking world — but which country to choose from? India, South America, Africa, Scandinavia? All had their candidates. Finally I selected a painting by the Japanese mouth-painter Iwao Adachi. The son of a steelworker in Osaka he lost both arms at the age of eleven when he accidentally touched a high voltage cable. His mother was so distraught at his accident that it probably contributed to her death soon afterwards. Young Adachi could only find work as a cleaner in a cinema until he finally managed to get a job as a store keeper. Meanwhile, without the benefit of tuition, he taught himself to paint in oils using a mouth-held brush and in 1962 his work was first hung in an exhibition in which he won a prize. He became a member of the Association in 1965 and over the years he has gone from strength to strength particularly with the landscapes he loves to paint.

I must confess that what endeared me to Adachi's work was his study of the fantastical castle of Neuschwanstein built by the brilliant but misunderstood Ludwig II of Bavaria who has always held my admiration. The picture is a spendid tribute by a Japanese artist to a romantic European king who preferred to give work to artists and craftsmen rather than soldiers.

Apart from artistic ability, the three things that the painters described in this book have in common are a complete lack of self-pity, immense enthusiasm for their work and — though they may wince at the word — courage.

In writing a book like this it is tempting to use such clichés as 'heartbreak and heroism', 'fantastic fortitude' or 'triumph over adversity' yet I will not make excuses for the word 'courage'. As for the 'canvases' the work reproduced here needs no wordy descriptions, it speaks for itself.

Marc Alexander

PAST MASTERS

*Painting became everything to me. By it I learned to
express myself in many subtle ways. Through it I made
articulate all that I saw and felt, all that went on inside
the mind that was housed within my useless body like a
prisoner in a cell looking out on a world that hadn't
become a reality to me.*

So wrote Christy Brown in his famous book *My Left Foot* that not long ago
was made into a film of the same name which won acclaim round the world.
Born in Dublin in 1932, Christy suffered from cerebral palsy which caused
paralysis in his arms and legs. In his biography he described growing up in a large
poverty-stricken family unable to do anything for himself, his mother being his
support.

In a moving passage he told how he clenched a stick of yellow chalk — his sisters
had been using it to do their sums — between the toes of his left foot and struggled
to print the letter A on the floor.

'That one letter...was my road to a new world, my key to mental freedom,' he
wrote later. 'It was to provide a source of relaxation to the tense, taut thing that was
me which panted for expression behind a twisted mouth.'

After this initial success he worked desperately to write with his foot. It was a highly
dramatic moment in the film when the first word he managed to print was MOTHER.

As Christy grew older and mastered the technique of using his foot as a hand he
turned to drawing and painting. When he was twelve the *Sunday Independent* ran
a Christmas painting competition in the form of a black and white scene from
Cinderella which had to be coloured in by young readers. Christy painstakingly
applied the colour — and won.

This success, minor though it might have seemed to an able-bodied child, was a
tremendous encouragement and from then on painting became a vital part of his
life, as his words quoted at the beginning testify. In many ways he was speaking
for hundreds of disabled artists who have struggled to express themselves by means
of brushes gripped in their teeth or held in their toes.

In another part of his book he wrote, 'Painting became the one great love in my
life, the main pivot of my concentration. I lived within the orbit of my paints and
brushes.'

Christy Brown found world fame as an author and a poet — what is not generally
known is that he received great assistance from the Association of Mouth and Foot
Painting Artists until his unexpected death in 1981. It was the German mouth-painter
Arnulf Erich Stegmann who went to Ireland to seek him and, finding him in a shed
at his parents' home in Dublin, invited him to join the self-help organisation he had
founded in the mid-fifties.

The Association was Erich Stegmann's dream of a world *partnership* of disabled
artists come true, a dream that had its beginnings when he was on the run from
the Nazis during the Second World War. And now he sought such artists with the

CEFISCHER   *Horses*   Watercolour

RICHARD HEXT   *Cows Drinking*   Watercolour

12

PIETER MOLEVELD   *Canal in Amsterdam*   Oil

CHRISTY BROWN   *Irish Landscape*   Oil   54 x 86 cm

tireless determination that radiated from him despite his own severe physical handicap. Those who met him always came away with the impression of vitality that surrounded him like a force field. Through some osmotic process he was able to infuse his confidence into those he was dedicated to helping, yet like all true confidence it was hard won.

Erich Stegmann had had to prove himself to himself again and again after he contracted poliomyelitis as a young child. Born the son of a bank clerk in Darmstadt in 1912, he was taken dangerously ill soon after the First World War broke out. The doctor broke it to his mother and father that their child was suffering from what was then known as Infantile Paralysis. As the result of the virus causing inflammation of the anterior horn cells of the spinal cord which govern muscle action it left its victims in varying degrees of paralysis.

When Erich survived the initial attack it became evident that he had lost the use of his arms and hands while his legs were also badly affected. He realized his disability when he watched his brothers and sisters romping and was powerless to join in with them.

Once in conversation with the German author J.H. Roesler Erich told him, 'I always remember when I was five years old how my mother put me to bed because of some mischief I was up to. You see, that was the way we were punished. We were not slapped when we had done wrong, but were undressed and without any arguments or explanations were put to bed. "You must stay in bed until I take you up!"

'The period we had to spend in bed was based on the gravity of the mischief we had done. It might be one hour or two hours. But it often happened, of course, that mother would forget to let us up again, perhaps because of the arrival of a visitor, or for some other reason. My brothers or sisters climbed out of bed themselves when their time was up but I could not stir without my mother's help — could not put on my clothes myself. Thus it turned out that I had to stay in bed beyond the time specified which I felt was most unjust! "Wicked mother! Wicked mother!" I used to rage helplessly, and it was from the experience that my resolution grew to become someone who could earn a lot of money so that I should not be dependent on anybody. This resolution, which I never gave up, made me succeed also in school.'

This thirst for independence was to remain the lodestone of Erich's life, first for himself and then for others. And at that remarkably early age he recognized that for the disabled money was the key to the things that the able-bodied took for granted — a home, a place in which to work, the means to travel, security.

When Erich was taken to school, his useless hands tucked neatly in his pockets, he sat stiffly and watched his fellow pupils working with pencils and crayons in their hands. If he felt like crying with frustration he held his tears back — his mother was not there to wipe them away. Instead he managed to manoeuvre the end of a pencil between his teeth and started trying to form his letters.

'I began to write and paint with the other children,' he recalled later in life. 'But I wanted to do better than the others. They wrote and painted with their hands — *my* hands were paralysed and I painted with my mouth so I wanted to prove to them that I could do it better than those who were not handicapped. And I did it better. In fact I did it so well that in 1927 I was accepted into the art school at the age of fifteen, and I was allowed to do live models at the age of sixteen, a privilege seldom granted to students of that age. I worked like mad and won a scholarship from the Lord Mayor of Nuremberg, where my parents now lived, to work for one year in the studio of a famous artist. The choice was left to me and I went to Erwin von Kormendy, a Hungarian painter.'

With each success Erich's confidence increased and by the time he was twenty-two he felt able to leave home. He shared a studio with his brother-in-law and set about earning his living as a professional painter. The life of an artist was something he had often imagined as a boy, and now it was made all the more sweet by his relationship with a girl named Bobby Hartman who was later to become his wife. Well aware that painting, like all forms of artistic expression, is not usually a safe profession from the financial standpoint, he set up his own publishing house.

But even the art world found it impossible to ignore politics in the 'thirties. It was a time of tension and stress, some feared the Communists and others the National Socialists led by the failed painter Adolf Hitler who, ten years after he was imprisoned for leading an unsuccessful rising in Munich, became the Chancellor.

From the start Erich Stegmann, with his fierce belief in individual freedom, was opposed to the Nazis and never failed to give tongue to his opposition. This made him officially an 'enemy of the state', and as such he was arrested at the end of 1934.

For the next fifteen months he had to endure gaol, not an easy situation for the able-bodied but ghastly for someone so physically handicapped, and as a piece of extra malice he was not allowed his paints. The result was that his physical condition deteriorated so badly that the medical officer responsible for the local prison decided that he should be transferred to the Munich prison at Ettstrasse which would not be such a strain on his health. And it was at Ettstrasse that he had an unexpected birthday present — the case against him was abandoned for lack of evidence. Years later he was to become an honorary member of the board of directors of an organization representing those who had been persecuted during the Nazi period — the *Vereinigung der Verfolgten des Naziregimes*.

Two months after his release he married Bobby and returned to publishing and painting. His experience of gaol did not deter him from continuing to oppose the Nazi Party and in 1944 he was forced to flee into hiding until the end of the Second World War. It was also the time that he and Bobby — with whom he shared two children — found that their marriage did not work.

In the chaos of early post-war Germany Erich sought to re-establish both his professional and private life. Some time after his divorce he married Traudi Billmeir, with whom he had two more children. He returned to painting and in the 'fifties was having one-man exhibitions in various capital cities.

Once when told how in a Rome art gallery the proprietor made a point of telling customers that his pictures exhibited there had been painted by mouth, Erich exploded, 'What difference does it make how a picture is painted? A painter does not mean only a pair of hands — he paints from his heart what his eyes see. The picture then wants to find friends. Pictures are like children who leave home. Nobody asks them whether their father has lost a foot or an arm. Why then should it arise with my pictures?'

Soon after the war Erich had 'discovered' the Adriatic island of Burano, a short boat-ride from Venice, which is noted for its traditional lace-making and old Venetian-style buildings. These houses with their vivid reflections trembling in the lagoon were an inspiration which brought him back to the island year after year. He bought a plot of land there and parked a caravan on it which became his summer residence. The view of him sitting in front of his easel, brush in mouth, became one of the commonplace sights of the island, and the only thing that may have struck the passers-by as odd was that he was the best-dressed artist ever to come to Venice.

In the beginning Erich painted out-of-doors as he did in his studio, in old comfortable clothing that was paint-spattered and gave off the smell of turps. One day when sitting at his easel to paint a street scene a crowd of instant art critics gathered round him as people will round an artist to see how close his painting is to the subject,

PETER SPENCER
The Girl with the Bracelet
Oil

ELIZABETH TWISTINGTON-HIGGINS   *Ballet Scene*   Tempera   39 x 52 cm

16

and it was seen that this artist — Good heavens! he has to paint with his mouth! — had his hat on the ground beside him. To the sympathetic onlookers this meant only one thing — and coins tinkled into the hat.

Although Erich perfectly understood their motives he felt he could not stand being the object of charity.

'Most people are so extremely considerate, they believe I am dependent on their help,' he said. 'That drives me mad.'

However, he had to face the fact that if he sat at his easel in public in his comfortable studio clothes the well-intended coins would continue to rain about him. His solution was to paint wearing a very expensive suit, the finest shirt money could buy and a bow tie. From then no one dared to offer a coin to this personification of sartorial elegance.

It is an amusing anecdote but it also illustrates Erich Stegmann's fundamental attitude which became the keystone of the Association of Mouth and Foot Painting Artists, the last thing he wanted was for people to think of it as a charity — it was to be a *partnership*.

Erich knew only too well the problems besetting disabled painters, many of whom were more disabled than he who could at least walk, and one of the main ones was the difficulty in making a living through artistic endeavour. Others, he knew, had the potential to become artists but were without the means to afford training or even in some cases the cost of paints, brushes and canvases. But with a partnership based on mutual help, and with a proper marketing programme, he believed correctly that it was possible for such artists to be self-supporting.

Having established the framework of the Association in 1956 with its headquarters in Vaduz, Liechtenstein, Erich roved the world in search of suitable members, and Christy Brown was just one of the many he sought out.

Despite his work as President and Founder of the Association, Erich Stegmann continued with his own art and when one looks at his work one is amazed at the variety of talent. There are his famous Burano paintings with their hot ochres, dark reds and greens and washed-out blues which immediately make one nostalgic for Venice. In contrast there are his delicate water-colours, his surreal works and abstracts, and his seemingly primitive works which radiate the strength of their creator.

He loved to experiment with every technique possible, ranging from litho work to prints made from wood blocks he incised with mouth-held tools. And, remarkable as it may seem, he used the same method with chisels to carve wood.

Erich Stegmann achieved the independent life that was his goal as a child, yet as well as success he experienced tragedy — the two children of his first marriage died in road accidents five years apart. He died in 1984 but, like John Brown in the American Civil War song, his spirit marches on. His inspiration is there every time a student or member of the Association he founded takes a brush in his or her teeth or toes.

Today the task of heading the Association is borne by the Swiss foot-painter Marlyse Tovae who has been the President since 1985.

When Erich Stegmann set up the Association of Mouth and Foot Painting Artists he knew that, if the scheme was to succeed, it would be essential to have members who could provide paintings for greetings cards that would equal, and indeed surpass, those already on the market. The last thing he wanted to do was publish work that would be bought out of pity — pity was an anathema to him. His aim was to help disabled artists, or those with artistic potential, to become self-sufficient but they had to be artists whose work was as competent as their able-bodied counterparts. There was no room in the Association for those without talent.

While there were a number of handicapped painters who would achieve a high enough standard after tuition, which in some cases might take several years, the Association needed those already proficient to supply the artwork which would lay the foundations for the enterprise. And it is thanks to the efforts of these original few that so many disabled artists members are able to live by the brush today.

The first member of the Association to be enrolled in England was Richard Hext who had been a mouth-painter since his teens. The son of an impoverished farm labourer, he was born in the closing decade of the last century in the small town of Ashburton which stands on the eastern edge of Dartmoor — the great stretch of wild country that was to have a life-long influence on him and inspire some of his best paintings.

Richard had been born disabled and when he was seven — around the time the Wright Brothers were making their pioneer flights — he had operations to straighten his legs and enable him to stand. Next he had treatment for his arms which resulted in them hanging neatly at his sides though he still had no use in them or in his twisted hands.

In the days before the First World War Social Security was merely the dream of liberal politicians and people in difficulties, whether through disability or unemployment, had to depend on relatives or get by as best they could. Young Richard did not want to be a liability yet what could he do? Unable to join in games with other boys, he found that he could amuse himself by drawing with a pencil held in his mouth. If this was his only ability he was determined to make the most of it and he managed to get himself accepted by the School of Art at nearby Newton Abbot. Here he remained for the next seven years after which he patiently continued to improve his technique at home.

He enjoyed painting still life studies and flower arrangements — subjects that were possible to tackle indoors — but always he was fascinated with the landscape of the brooding moor.

In 1923 Richard felt that at last he had reached a satisfactory standard with an oil painting of two Pekingese looking over a wall and this he sent as a gift to Queen Alexandra because of her interest in these lively little dogs.

Writing her thanks, the dowager queen said that she had placed the painting in a place where she would often see it at Sandringham. The letter pleased him so much that he had it framed and placed above the fireplace where it remained for the rest of his life.

After his time in Newton Abbot Richard only ventured twice out of Ashburton where he lived with his mother in their small house. A writer who visited his home expressed amazement that he was able to paint such vivid pictures in the tiny sunless room in which he worked.

It seems the answer was that he could hold colour in his memory, especially after a friend would drive him out on to Dartmoor to sketch, and his drab home surroundings had no effect on the masterpieces that materialized on his canvas.

Richard sent his paintings to America where a cousin sold them for him but the return was pitifully small for the effort he put into his work, often painting a picture a day. His only recreations were his Friday nights at the Ashburton Social Club and the keeping of prize pigeons. Four years in succession he won the Torns Cup for carrier-pigeon breeding.

In 1953 he repeated his gesture of sending a painting to a queen — this time it was a coronation gift to Elizabeth II who repeated the gesture of her great-grandmother by sending him a graceful letter of thanks. The picture was a study of a stone bridge on the River Dart and is believed to have been the best piece of work he ever did.

A modest, pleasant man, Richard Hext continued to paint without the recognition or financial reward he deserved until Erich Stegmann invited him to joint the Mouth and Foot Painting Artists in the year of its inauguration to paint scenes for some of the greetings cards which were to finance the Association. At last he had an income commensurate with his ability and a guarantee of comfort for the rest of his life, yet he was content to remain in the house he had always lived in. He was particularly happy that he could now afford to make life easier for his mother who had devoted herself to looking after him — and happy, too, to remain close to Dartmoor which had provided him with so much inspiration.

One of the original members of the Association whose work was an important factor in its establishment was Carl Fischer-Cefischer who, unlike Richard Hext, was already well known when he joined it. He was a professional artist in Germany before the Second World War and after it broke out he was called up for military service and sent to Prague. In 1944 he was due for leave and he sent a telegram to his wife in Amorbach, 'The day after tomorrow I will be with you. Love, Carl.'

The train which was taking him home had just pulled into the station at Fulda when an air raid warning sounded. Passengers leapt from the carriages and raced towards the air raid shelter outside the station as the first bombs began to explode. Carl threw himself to the ground and instinctively raised his hands to protect his head. A bomb burst close by and one of its splinters amputated both his arms.

When the news reached his wife she had only one thought and that was to be at his side. Travel at that stage of the war was almost impossible for civilians but nothing could deter her. She walked, hitched rides on trucks and somehow managed to get aboard a troop train only to be put off whenever the military police spotted her — and pulled on board again by the soldiers when the MPs had gone. After three days she reached the hospital where her husband lay racked both by physical agony and agony of mind — if he survived what future could there be for an artist without arms?

After three weeks, during which his wife never left his bedside, Carl's despair lifted. If his wife was so happy that he was still alive even though maimed, he should rejoice that he had such loving support. And with his change of mood the doctors announced that his injuries were healing faster than they thought possible.

One morning his wife said to him, 'Carl, do you remember that holiday we had before the war in Mittenwald and the man we saw painting in the market square?'

'You mean the crippled one who held the brush in his mouth?'

'Yes. He seemed so full of life when he talked to us, and he managed to paint so well....'

'All right,' said Carl. 'I will give this mouth-painting a month's trial.'

Well aware that his future depended on mastering this new technique he drove himself desperately to regain his old skill. When he was finally satisfied that he had done so he returned to the office of the West German magazine for which he used to work and here he introduced a new pictorial character known as Tom Cat Oscar who was always attired in distinctive black trousers, red-striped jumper and a blue tie. The comic adventures and domestic tribulations of Tom Cat Oscar, modelled by Carl's pet white and ginger cat, proved immensely popular not only in the magazine but in several books which sold over a million copies.

One day in Vaduz Carl Fischer-Cefischer had a meeting with the disabled artist he had watched years earlier in Mittenwald — Erich Stegmann. And as a result he became one of the Association's first members.

Another professional artist invited by Erich Stegmann to join his fledgling organisation was Pieter Moleveld, the son of a Dutch architect, who was completing his art studies when Holland was invaded at the onset of the Second World War.

Food soon became in short supply but the Moleveld family sometimes had extra because Pieter was asked by grocers to design food advertisements to put in their windows in lieu of the real thing. He was adamant that he could not paint cheeses, hams, baskets of eggs and so on unless he had models to work from, and as some of his commissions came from the royal victuallers he was suitably supplied.

The family also eked out their rations by growing huge quantities of French beans. When the crop was ready it was traditional for friends to take part in the picking and preserving, a task largely done by women because towards the end of the war most men had been drafted to work in Germany. Pieter was about to go to an optics factory when bean-picking time came around. Among those present for the harvest was a family friend with her daughter Margarethe who worked alongside Pieter. The two young people had a happy day together, and in the evening when he saw her home he asked her if she would model for him.

'I was afraid at the time that it would be immoral,' Margarethe admitted much later. In reality it was not immoral but hard work as Pieter painted her over and over again until he plucked up enough courage to propose. After that they celebrated each anniversary of their wedding with a meal in which French beans were the main ingredient.

When peace returned to Europe Pieter became well-known as a painter at the Haager School, he and Margarethe had three children and when their eldest was ten years old they planned to get a larger apartment in which Pieter would have a more spacious studio.

These plans were dashed in September 1956 when Pieter was suddenly taken ill and within hours poliomyelitis was diagnosed. In the hospital Margarethe had to give her consent for a tracheal operation to be performed in order for him to breathe by means of artificial respiration. Thanks to this surgery he survived but was left with his limbs paralysed and his mind darkened by depression — he felt his career as an artist was over and with it his means of supporting his family.

After a year in which he found it very difficult to adjust to his new condition, it was suggested, that as he still had a little movement in his foot, he might try painting with a brush held in his toes. He was reluctant to try until his old teacher Pieter van Boreel encouraged him. At first Pieter was even more depressed because he found it impossible to manipulate the brush and he protested that he felt like a three-year-old trying to paint.

Pieter van Boreel made him persevere and finally he succeeded in producing a foot painting which was as good as the paintings he had done in the days when he enjoyed good health. Now he could only breathe normally for two hours a day, the rest of the time he had to rely on oxygen which he received from hospital-supplied cylinders through a respiratory device implanted near his larynx.

It was impossible for him to return to the Haager School but after Erich Stegmann had asked him to paint for the Association he was able to earn his living at home, his pictures of evocative Dutch landscapes setting a standard of excellence for the cards produced by the new organisation.

Many other painters who came after Richard Hext, Carl Fischer-Cefischer and Pieter Moleveld have contributed greatly to the growth of the Association of Mouth and Foot Painting Artists but no retrospective chapter would be complete without mention of Peter Spencer MBE who did so much to further the organisation.

He achieved much as an artist and a great deal outside the world of art, and if he owed a lot to the Association the Association came to owe a lot to him. Yet in the beginning, unlike the other artists described in this book, he was not regarded as talented enough to be taken on as a student. After sending in some of his paintings he received the following reply: 'Thank you for sending us samples of your work but we regret that your paintings do not come up to the standard we require for publication.'

Peter Spencer was fifteen and a pupil of Oldershaw Grammar School in Wallasey in what is now designated Merseyside at the outbreak of the Second World War. When the Air Training Corps was formed in Wallasey he enthusiastically joined 273 Squadron. Later he enlisted in the RAF and in the summer of 1943 he sailed out of Liverpool bound for the No 5 British Flying Training School at Clewiston in Florida.

After wartime Britain America was a revelation to the young airmen; no blackout, no shortage of food and a dizzy social life as hospitable Americans wanted to entertain the boys who were going to fly against Hitler. But, as Peter told the author some time ago, there was a dark side to the sunshine life. The cadets were warned that two of their number had been killed on each course.

'It was an uncomfortable feeling to think that two of us might not make it — that it might be me in a training crash,' he said. 'And sure enough two of our chaps did get killed. Altogether over thirty RAF cadets died during training at Clewiston, and there is a special cemetery for them where there is a ceremony of remembrance held every year.'

Peter won his 'Wings' in February 1944 and returned to Britain to fly Dakotas of Transport Command. He began operational flying in September with 512 Squadron of 46 Group Transport Command at Broadwell in Oxfordshire. He and his crew of three flew their Dakota on regular runs across the Channel to carry supplies to the forward units in the invasion of France. In February of the following year he was promoted to Flight Sergeant and soon he was flying to the Rhine in support of the crossing there, returning with his aircraft scarred by anti-aircraft flak.

On 27 March Peter had a rest day but an urgent job came up and he volunteered to fly four officers to Rheims in an Anson aircraft. As the truck took them out to their plane on the tarmac a taxi-ing Mosquito bomber caught the vehicle with its starboard propeller and Peter's right arm was shorn off.

When he came round in hospital he realized that not only had he lost one arm but the other was paralysed. The first thought that came into his head was 'I'll never play the piano again.' The pain was indescribable and could only be held at bay with injections of morphine.

In order to rehabilitate him when he came out of hospital the Air Ministry department dealing with the resettlement of airmen arranged for him to go to the Central School of Speech Training and Dramatic Art in London in order for him to try for a job with the BBC as an announcer. It was an imaginative idea but one thing had been overlooked until the audition — in his condition it was impossible for him to handle the pages of a script or flick the necessary switches.

Returning to his parents' home in Wallasey Peter, now twenty-four and on a hundred percent war disability pension of £2 4s 0d. a week, began giving elocution lessons. Then, in July 1950, he met the girl he was destined to marry. One day he went for a walk to the New Brighton pier where a show called 'Happy Time' was being performed in the open-air theatre, and as he approached it he saw a girl on the stage singing 'O My Beloved Father'. Her looks and vitality had a great impact on Peter while June Lynette, when she left the stage, carried the mental picture of a handsome young man with dark curling hair who had not taken his eyes off her during the performance. And she was not at all surprised that he was waiting for her after the show.

It was only then that she realized that the right sleeve of his jacket was empty. Peter explained simply that he had not only lost one arm but also the use of the other.

June's reaction could not have been better — she merely said, 'How interesting.' And agreed to meet him that evening.

In the bar of the Grand Hotel June raised his glass to his lips for him as though she had known him for ages — indeed, in a curious way she felt she had — and so their romance began.

What worried Peter was the thought that if she agreed to marry him, how could he provide for her, and perhaps a family, on a disability pension supplemented by what he could earn teaching elocution? When he finally raised this she brushed it aside.

'I was sent to marry and look after you,' she said. 'I have always known that.'

They married on 12 December 1951 in St Nicholas's Church in Wallasey.

It was through one of *Ripley's Believe It or Not* cartoon features that Peter first learned of Erich Stegmann, a disabled German artist who painted by holding a brush in his mouth. The story fascinated Peter and he tried the technique. It was far more difficult than he had expected but he was filled with an ambition to emulate Stegmann. Towards Christmas he came across some cards published by the Association of Mouth and Foot Painting Artists and, thinking he might be on the brink of a new career, he sent off six paintings and waited eagerly for the verdict. When it came it was to turn him down.

While the Association did not feel his standard was high enough, he was not forgotten and some months later he was invited to an exhibition of members' work. And there he came face-to-face with the man who he had learned about through Ripley — Erich Stegmann. Through an interpreter the founder of the Association repeated that while Peter's work showed talent it was not sufficiently developed, and then added, 'I suggest that you attend art school and we will give you a scholarship to cover the cost of your tuition and materials.'

Peter took a course at the Wallasey School of Art. His determination to make painting a career was given a new impetus when his son Robin was born in 1958 — their second child Jill Rosemary arrived in 1962 — and next year any doubts he had about providing for his family ended when at an Association conference in Edinburgh it was announced that he had been given full membership.

Apart from the financial benefits which came with membership, it strengthened Peter's confidence in other directions. In 1960 he stood for the local council, won the Marlowe Ward and held it with an ever-increasing majority for the next fourteen years; he served as Chairman of the Wallasey Arts Society and President and Chairman of the Merseyside Branch of the British Limbless Ex-Servicemen's Association. Finding that he could speak well and amusingly in public he took on the job of public relations officer for the Association which entailed travelling overseas to promote the work of his fellow artists.

In 1970 Peter's biography *No Man An Island* by Eileen Waugh, with a foreword by Douglas Bader, became a best seller and when it was translated into French the humanitarian society *Merite et Devouement Francais* awarded him *Le Croix de Commandeur* for 'exceptional services to humanity' through the example he gave to others in adversity.

Peter's best moment came in 1980 when he went to Buckingham Palace to be invested with the MBE. As Her Majesty realized that she could not shake hands with him she placed her hand on his left sleeve before pinning the award on his lapel.

Two years later Peter became a Deputy Lieutenant of the County of Merseyside and because many of his paintings reflected his early love of flying, the Guild of Aviation Artists elected him as Associate Member. Yet no matter how busy Peter was he continued painting and right up to his death in 1987 he worked enthusiastically to further the cause of the Association.

Writing of Peter's painting, the art historian Dr Richard Hiepe said, 'His passion for flying, from which he was barred by his accident, is expressed in his magically overdrawn "portraits" of the giant aeroplanes of the jet age. They are not photographic descriptions, but homages to a novel kind of beauty.'

Without doubt Elizabeth Twistington Higgins was the best known of Britain's mouth painters — and the most handicapped. Her story has been told on the *This Is Your Life* programme and in books, including her own *Still Life* and the biography *The Dance Goes On*. An hour-long film of the same name has been shown several times on British television and on many television channels around the world. Named the Best Documentary of 1980 by the magazine *Films and Filming*, it endeavoured to tell the story of Elizabeth's past life and show her at work not only at her specially designed easel but also putting her remarkable ballet group the Chelmsford Dancers through their graceful paces.

Narrated by Rudolf Nureyev, the film used still photographs to tell the story of Elizabeth's early life. When the Second World War began the Twistington Higgins family returned from holiday to their home in Highgate, London, to find that the only school left open was a dancing academy. Elizabeth, Brighid and Alison, the three daughters of Thomas Twistington Higgins, a celebrated pioneer of children's surgery, were enrolled and enjoyed two hours of dancing practice before ordinary lessons every morning.

For Elizabeth the new regime was a delight as she had dreamed of a career as a ballet dancer ever since the age of fourteen after being taken to Sadler's Wells for a magical performance of *Les Sylphides* by her brother. Later when she mentioned her ambition to her father he replied with the infuriating logic of adults that she must finish her normal education before considering such an insecure career. But when she matriculated he agreed that she could apply for training at Sadler's Wells.

After a short try-out period Elizabeth's high hopes were dashed when she was told from a physical point of view she was not suited for the Sadler's Wells company. If her hopes were dashed they were not extinguished, and she went to a school run by the famous Cone Sisters — known today as The Arts Educational School — where she earned her Advanced Ballet certificate and won the prestigious Solo Seal in 1945 after which she became a teacher at the school.

Elizabeth enjoyed teaching and later became known as the Penny Ballerina when she taught pre-school children at Coram's Fields, the well known playground in Bloomsbury, and organized 'penny concerts' at which musicians from the Royal Academy of Music gave up Saturday mornings to perform for the local children.

Meanwhile she auditioned for and was accepted as a member of the musical *Song of Norway* at the Palace Theatre in Shaftesbury Avenue which ran for fourteen months, after which she did film and television work, and took part in a pantomime at the London Palladium. Next she successfully auditioned for Ivor Novello's *King's Rhapsody* in which she danced until the musical closed several months after the death of Novello in 1951.

By now Elizabeth found that teaching gave her more satisfaction than performing, and she started her own classes at the Art Workers' Guild Hall in London's Queen Square, opposite the National Hospital for Nervous Diseases. During the 1953 poliomyelitis epidemic it was to this hospital that Elizabeth was rushed by ambulance after she had been taken ill at her parents' home in Mongeham, Kent. Here polio was diagnosed and in Elizabeth's words 'they whizzed me out of the ward, wheeled me along seemingly endless corridors to a room on Ward 12 where I was shoved in an iron lung, and that was that!'

When the film on Elizabeth's life came to be made the problem was how to portray the onset of the illness that completely paralysed her apart from a very slight movement in her right hand. The idea of using an actress to play Elizabeth's part was discarded, instead it was decided to recreate the episode by showing an ambulance racing into Queen Square, the hospital staff taking the stretcher inside and ending at the iron lung. The camera was to be mounted on the stretcher so that the viewers would see everything as Elizabeth saw it that long-ago day and have the sensation of being slid into the coffin-like breathing machine.

And here the film team experienced one of the many remarkable coincidences that occurred during the making of *The Dance Goes On*. Over a quarter of a century had passed since Elizabeth had been driven to the National Hospital — where did one get an ambulance of the 'fifties from?

It was found that there is an Ambulance Museum and it could provide a suitable vehicle with driver. After the ambulance and arrival had been filmed in Queen Square, the driver remarked that out of all the ambulances that had been on the road in 1953 this was the actual one that had brought Elizabeth up from Kent.

When asked how he could be sure, he replied that the driver of the ambulance had joined the staff of the Ambulance Museum and had passed on the anecdote — he would have driven the vehicle himself only he happened to be retiring that very day.

Iron lungs, too, had changed and the helpful authorities at the National Hospital tried to discover if there was an old model still in existence. They located one at the Royal National Orthopaedic Hospital in Stanmore and when the film crew arrived there they were told that this surviving lung had originally come from the National Hospital and would have been the one used by Elizabeth. As more coincidences followed the crew began to expect a new one every day, even such minor examples as a hire-car driver remarking out of the blue that he had lived next door to the Twistington Higgins family as a child.

In the National Hospital for Nervous Diseases Elizabeth remained very ill for a long time, dependent for life on the iron lung whose varying pressure kept her lungs working. The children she taught lit candles for her in the local Roman Catholic church and Margot Fonteyn, whose marriage took place at this time, sent her a bridal bouquet — one of the many tokens of love that Elizabeth received from her friends in the ballet world.

Physiotherapists tried to restore Elizabeth's neck muscles so that she could use them to consciously draw air into her lungs and twenty-seven months after she had been stricken she was able to remain outside the lung for up to four hours. Her every breath was performed by a deliberate mental command to the accessory breathing muscles in her neck — a process known as 'frog' breathing — and these commands had to be given *consciously* no matter what else she had to think about. She once described the process to the author as like having two tunes running through her head simultaneously. And because breathing was a conscious effort for Elizabeth she had to sleep in an iron lung each night.

A great moment in her life came when she left the hospital for her first brief outing in Queen Square. Taken from the lung, she was laid on a trolley from the operating theatre and escorted by two nurses, a physiotherapist and a doctor, she was wheeled round the square while from every window of the hospital waving hands showed that both patients and staff shared her triumph.

From the National Hospital Elizabeth went to the Royal National Orthopaedic Hospital in Stanmore; later she was able to stay with her parents thanks to a portable cuirass-type respirator and the help of a visiting physiotherapist and district nurse.

24

But a severe winter ended this for fear that storm would bring down the electricity cables and her respirator would go dead. On several occasions this happened and her parents had to hurriedly take her out of her lung so she could begin 'frog' breathing. These alarming incidents made her realize that her being at home was becoming too difficult for her mother and father and regretfully she planned to become hospitalized again.

In 1957 she was moved from her home to the British Polio Fellowship Hostel. Here there were no staff members on duty during the afternoons which Elizabeth found frustrating because there was no one to turn the pages of her book. Other patients managed this with mouthsticks, and Elizabeth wondered whether it would be possible for her to hold one in her teeth and breathe at the same time. After a lot of effort Elizabeth mastered the stick without it affecting her breathing and the turning of a page became the first thing she was able to do for herself for four years.

The mouthstick was the precursor of the mouth-held paintbrush. One of the Friends of the Hostel named Rosie suggested Elizabeth might pass some of the time by painting and, despite her first almost hilarious attempts when paint splattered everywhere, Elizabeth found it fun. Like some other severely disabled people whose condition makes them difficult to be categorized, Elizabeth was then transferred again, this time to the Dover Isolation Hospital, and here a breakthrough in her painting came when she took regular lessons with a local art teacher named Rosemary Howard.

'It took Elizabeth nine months to master the technique of loading her brush with paint,' Rosemary told the author. 'She could not move her head forward very far so the board had to be moved into the orbit of her brush. Sometimes she would do a pleasing sketch and then, quite unexpectedly, jerk. The brush would slither down and all that effort would be wasted.'

As Elizabeth's skill progressed and she began to paint her famous ballet pictures. Rosemary commented later, 'Obviously, inside herself she was dancing with those figures. When they were poised on one foot I felt she was somehow part of them; it was *her* arms that were extended, and *she* was on the stage under the lights.'

Elizabeth's father used a reproduction of one of her paintings for a Christmas card in 1958 and this led to her being interviewed by a journalist from a London paper, and his story in turn led to Elizabeth's first exhibition held at the Dover School of Art.

Word of Elizabeth's talent spread and in 1961 fifty of her paintings were used in coloured panels in the Queen's reception room during the Festival Ballet's Christmas season at the Royal Festival Hall. The following year she appeared on *This Is Your Life*. After the programme there was such a demand for her pictures that soon she had none left to sell, and with this success came the dream of leading an independent life again. It was a dream that became a reality after she was asked to join the Association of Mouth and Foot Painting Artists.

The film was able to demonstrate what independence meant to Elizabeth by showing a day in her life, starting at the Broomfield Hospital in Chelmsford where she had to spend every night in an iron lung. Once she had been prepared for the day Elizabeth was taken by her own ambulance to her house. A rota of helpers ensured that she was properly cared for while on her wheelchair was mounted a POSM — Patient Operated Selector Mechanism. By blowing into a plastic mouthpiece Elizabeth was able to activate the device to summon her helper, control the temperature and lighting and make calls on the telephone.

Because Elizabeth's neck movement was so restricted and therefore did not allow her much range on her canvas when painting, a special motorized easel was made for her by Doug Adams, an engineer whose hobby is designing equipment for the disabled. Apart from her neck muscles Elizabeth's only movement was in a finger in her right hand. At the slightest pressure on micro switches set in a plastic cast the easel's board moved up and down and sideways.

Apart from her art work Elizabeth wrote a book on her experiences entitled *Still Life* which was published in 1969. For this she used an electric typewriter which she also operated with her right hand positioned over the keyboard in a special sling attached to an overhead support.

But the most remarkable of her achievements was her return to ballet teaching. Soon after Elizabeth had settled into the routine of her new home Joan Weston, the honorary director and founder of the Chelmsford Ballet Company, asked if she would be interested in producing a tarantella for eight girls in a forthcoming production. Despite inward misgiving Elizabeth accepted the challenge.

'I shall never forget how I met Elizabeth,' recalls one of the Chelmsford Ballet dancers involved. 'I was there for some casting auditions and she was coming to see the dancers and choose those she wanted. At that time I knew nothing about her, except that she was a lady in a wheelchair and everybody spoke with great reverence and in hushed voices. "Oh, that's Miss Twistington Higgins coming..." And there she was. All the doors were opened wide and some of us helped to lift her wheelchair up three steps into the studio. Everyone stood around in awed silence. All the girls stopped chattering, and this very frail, thin person started to address us...'

The tarantella was a great success and followed in 1971 with Elizabeth arranging dance sequences for an experimental Eucharist in Chelmsford Cathedral. The performance was so moving that many members of the congregation were in tears — and Elizabeth knew that she wanted to continue with liturgical ballet.

To this end she formed her own ballet company, the Chelmsford Dancers, who for the next eleven years performed all over the country in cathedrals, churches, hospitals and even in prisons. Helped by her assistant director Sheila Large, Elizabeth managed to do everything, from the choreography to designing the costumes with her mouth-held brush. A practice session of Elizabeth's dancers was filmed, with Elizabeth using a POSM-operated tape recorder to provide the music, and then the camera was taken to All Souls in Langham Place, London, where a glorious performance was recorded.

Ballet work did not replace Elizabeth's art work for the Association of Mouth and Foot Painting Artists, and in 1977 she was taken to Buckingham Palace to receive from Her Majesty the Queen the order of the MBE in recognition of her skill as a painter.

Elizabeth described the moment when she was wheeled forward and the Queen stepped down from her dais and placed the order on the little hook which had been attached to her blouse for the purpose thus, 'Her Majesty is very petite, being little higher than I was sitting in my wheelchair. Her voice was soft and melodious, and she seemed to generate kindliness. And how well she must have done her homework. That morning nearly two hundred people came before her and only the name of the recipient was announced with no hint as to what they were being honoured for. Yet Her Majesty had words for everybody, and when it was my turn she had a long talk to me about my painting. Then, by way of dismissal, she said, "I do hope this outing has not tired you too much." The page took control of the wheelchair and I was rolled away a Member of the British Empire.'

Four years after the film on Elizabeth's life was shown on television several of the Chelmsford Dancers could no longer continue due to domestic and career reasons and Elizabeth, rather than let the company's standards drop, decided it was best 'to go out on a high'.

Elizabeth died suddenly and without pain in September 1990 at her home in

Chelmsford. When working on the film of her life the author asked her what she regarded as her ultimate goal to which she answered, 'I should think a nice little dance in Heaven.' If anyone deserved such a modest reward it is Elizabeth and no doubt for her the dance goes on.

ALBERT BAKER

The gift of self respect

It is sometimes extraordinary how beauty can be born out of ugliness. There can be no argument that there was a lot of ugliness in Albert Baker's early life yet if you watch Albert paint a rose before your eyes — as he often does at demonstrations — you will see beauty materialize.

Thankfully the public's attitude towards disabled people has changed greatly since the years before the Second World War when Albert was mocked for his appearance, having been born with deformed feet and without the use of his arms or legs. And added to the burden of disability was a disturbed home life.

'My father was very cruel to my mother,' Albert recalls. 'Even in those days when I was very small I sensed how unhappy she was.'

A man of very quick and violent temper, Albert's father kept something in the coal cellar which filled the little boy with dread. If Albert cried with pain it was brought out — a cane.

When Albert was three years old he went for assessment of his disability in St Thomas's Hospital, London, and this was the beginning of an institutionalized life. From St Thomas's he went to the Royal National Orthopaedic Hospital at Stanmore and then on to St Nicholas' and St Martin's Orthopaedic Hospital where he remained until he was fourteen.

Although there was a special school associated with the hospital it was of little benefit to Albert whose education was frequently interrupted by surgical operations which meant that during childhood he was constantly in pain. It seemed there was only one ray of light in those dark days — drawing and painting which he taught himself by holding a pencil or brush in his mouth.

In the hope that he might be able to learn a trade which he could follow despite his physical difficulties Albert was taken to a special school in Seaford on the Sussex coast in 1936. After three months it was recognized that he was far too handicapped for anything the school could teach him and he was sent to a hospital in Dartford where he had to suffer more operations.

'I think a lot of my operations were exploratory,' Albert says today. 'My mother told me a few months before she died that she had signed a paper giving them blanket permission to do whatever they thought necessary, and this allowed them to experiment. After an operation on each wrist my hands were twice as bad as they had been before and I was left more dependent on people doing things for me.'

When the series of operations came to an end Albert was fitted with leg irons and surgical boots. Although the irons cut into his flesh when he attempted to move, he persevered in learning to walk by leaning himself against a wall and pushing himself along. Although he fell countless times he finally managed to cross a room under his own power — 'waddle across it' to use his own words.

Albert was now seventeen. The authorities asked his mother if she would look after him at home but financial difficulties forced her to live on public assistance and the ten shillings a week she received was not enough to allow her to keep Albert — there was no cash help for the disabled before the Second World War.

'The only place for me to go was the workhouse which was run under the Poor Law system which was still in operation at that time,' Albert explains.

Understandably distressed at the plight of her son, Albert's mother pleaded with the authorities not to confine him in a room full of old men and as a special favour he was permitted to stay in a wing of the workhouse that was used as a hospital ward. It was better than being with the geriatrics but it was still a very depressing time for the young man. During his three years' stay there, Albert only left the workhouse once — to a concert given by boys from Dr Barnardo's Home.

One of the things that greatly upset Albert was the fact that he was frequently teased for being a cripple.

'I could manage to waddle along in those days and the others used to make fun of me over that,' he says. 'They called me Albert Ramsbottom, not because of Stanley Holloway's famous monologue about Albert and the Lion but because my backside stuck out when I walked. It was started by a member of the staff who should have known better. People can be cruel and being very sensitive made it worse for me.'

Workhouse days ended in 1939 when Albert was sent to Yorkshire to stay in a home 'for incurables and cripples' run by monks who believed in a strict regime for their charges. In those days Albert was able to walk for about a mile — an ability he later lost — and it was his delight to escape into the countryside. On one occasion, when visiting the local village, he was seen passing the time of day with a female villager, and when he returned to the home he was told that if he spoke to women in the future he would be banished.

His interest in art remained unabated despite the unnatural life he was forced to lead for the next fourteen years. Inspired by the beauty of the surrounding landscape he painted scenic postcards, producing several mouth-painted cards a week which he sold for a shilling each. He would have liked to have worked on larger format pictures but the home was always short of staff and there was no one to help him to set up the necessary equipment for 'real' painting. Rather than encouragement Albert found the opposite — it was regarded as a joke by other inmates to pour water over his cards.

In the end Albert could stand it no longer. Because of a lack of attendants to help the patients, those who had some mobility once they were up now had to remain in bed twenty-four hours a day. In reply to his desperate letters, Albert's mother agreed to look after him and with heart-felt relief he returned to London.

At last things began to improve. No longer in the 'incurable and crippled' class, Albert became an outpatient at King's College Hospital in Denmark Hill where occupational therapy enabled him to do more for himself. He also continued to sell his mouth-painted postcards though he earned little enough from them when each represented a full day's work.

For three years Albert was able to stay with his mother but with the weight of the years she found it more and more difficult to manage. Finally it was decided that Albert should reside at Le Court in Hampshire which was the first home set up by Group Captain Leonard Cheshire VC OM. For someone whose life had been as bleak and painful as Albert's, Le Court was like a haven after a long and ardous journey. His only reservation was that there was not enough money to be made out of selling original postcards for him to pay for his keep himself, something he felt deeply.

Meanwhile word had reached Erich Stegmann that there was a mouth painter somewhere in England who painted postcards. Continuously in search of disabled artists, or potential artists, Erich began a search for Albert but it was some time before the Association tracked him down to Le Court. When this happened his work was evaluated in the usual way and he was enrolled as a student which meant that he was able to have a tutor to give him art lessons. After the long years of deprivation he had the joy of being able to afford proper paints and brushes.

Four years later Albert became a full member of the Association which not only gave him financial independence but experiences that in his wildest day dreams he never imagined would come his way. He discovered the magic of travel, enjoying holidays in France and America and attending Delegates' Conferences held in different countries by the Association. For local travel he was able to save up to buy an estate car in which to be driven and later an ambulance fitted with an electric hoist to make it easy for him to get aboard in his wheelchair.

But best of all the benefits is the thought that he can live entirely by his own efforts. And because of his interest in young people — Albert is often seen with a crowd of children round his easel watching while he paints — he was delighted when he was appointed as one of the governors of the Church of England primary school at Greatham, Hampshire, again something that once seemed so unlikely for a man who never received proper schooling.

Today Albert lives happily in his own home in Greatham, a just reward for all his long years of endeavour, yet he has no intention of resting on his laurels despite the fact that he is past retirement age. The pictures he continues to paint are some of the most popular marketed as greeting cards by the Association, exhibitions of his work are held regularly and he retains his interest in the community about him. A recent story in a local newspaper told how a vital extension to the Greatham Village Hall for its playgroup, which had been under the threat of closure, had been completed by a donation of £4000 from the popular artist Albert Baker — and what must have pleased Albert when he read the item was the fact that no one had thought it necessary to mention that he was a disabled artist.

Albert has never forgotten Erich Stegmann and the way he sought him, and he says, 'Stegmann used his genius for the good of others. What more charitable act can you do than restore a man's faith and confidence in himself or give it to him if he has lacked it before? In the past I felt so useless that I thought of doing away with myself but he gave me the gift of self respect which I had never known before.'

ALBERT BAKER   *Blossoms with Butterflies*   Watercolour

ALBERT BAKER   *Summer Landscape*   Oil

ALBERT BAKER   *Wild Ducks*   Watercolour   15 x 22 cm

ALBERT BAKER   *Church in the Snow*   Tempera

WENDY BARBER   *Santa Claus with Rucksack*   Watercolour   25 x 21 cm

WENDY BARBER   *Santa Claus*   Watercolour   16 x 16 cm

WENDY BARBER   *Candles*   Watercolour   29 x 21 cm

WENDY BARBER   *Snowman with Walking Stick*   Watercolour   13 x 14 cm

Overleaf:
GLENN BARNETT
Outback Road
Oil   56 x 76 cm

GLENN BARNETT
Dusk
Oil

GLENN BARNETT   *Sailing Boat*   Oil   33 x 51 cm

40

JOHN BUNCE   *Remembrance*   Watercolour   42 x 30 cm

FLORENCE BUNN
Flowers
Painted on Ceramics

FLORENCE BUNN
Roses
Watercolour

JOHN BUNCE
Beaver
Tempera   35 x 25 cm

JOHN BUNCE
Two Kittens
Tempera   37 x 27 cm

FLORENCE BUNN
Winter Landscape
Ceramic Tile   20 x 15 cm

FLORENCE BUNN
Candle Design
Watercolour   15 x 15 cm

JOHN BUTLER   *Sunday Outing — Newcastle, 1903*   Oil   25 x 35 cm

JOHN BUTLER   *Quiet Walk*   Oil   20 x 24 cm

JOHN BUTLER
Springbok
Watercolour   36 x 27 cm

JOHN BUTLER   *The Long Haul*   Oil   20 x 24 cm

STEVEN CHAMBERS   *Morning Mist*   Watercolour   53 x 38 cm

JOY CLARKE
Brook Landscape
Watercolour   16 x 11 cm

JOY CLARKE
Spring Flowers
Watercolour   23 x 16 cm

WENDY BARBER

'I have to cope. There is no choice.'

Wendy Barber lives alone in a bungalow called the Beehive, in the window of which is a sign announcing 'Honey for sale' — a sign which is puzzling to anyone who arrives at the house in search of a disabled artist. Yet the keeping of bees is just one of the many facets of Wendy's extraordinary life, reflecting her love of nature which in turn is reflected in her paintings produced by a brush held painfully in her mouth.

Wendy's interest in art was fostered early by her father, a Fleet Street printer and later in life a television engineer whose hobby was pencil drawing, and this was furthered when she attended art school. At the age of nineteen she married and two years later gave birth to her son Matthew. Shortly afterwards it was found that she was suffering from cancer of the throat and neck.

Wendy's mother looked after the baby while she spent the first of many long periods in hospital.

'The specialist told me that I was more likely to die than live,' Wendy recalls, 'but after three months in hospital receiving intensive treatment and major surgery I was allowed home two days before Matthew's first birthday. At that time my greatest anxiety was fearing my husband would not be able to cope with the cancer. In fact he left me when Matthew was two years old.

'The way I survived was not to think of negative things, and I needed to survive for Matthew's sake. If you have a child there's a bond there, and in between my times in hospital I tried to stay as well as I could so I could carry on looking after him. Then, three years after I had been told I had cancer, Matthew contracted meningitis. I did not have time to think about my illness, all I could think was, "I have to cope. There is no choice." And it was at times like that when you find you have strengths that you didn't know you had.'

The illness left the little boy brain-damaged with severe deafness and epilepsy, yet thanks to Wendy's devotion he has grown up to be a fine young man who is able to lead an independent life and gives much of his free time to voluntary work with the Lions.

After seven years of treatment which included three major operations Wendy was declared clear of cancer. It had been an almost miraculous recovery and yet she did not feel as well as she ought. Before long she began losing her balance and falling over, and soon she could only move about like a young child sliding on its bottom. Then it was discovered that she was a victim of multiple sclerosis, the diagnosis of which had been delayed because all her symptoms had been put down to the cancer.

Today Wendy is paralysed from the neck down and suffers a great deal of pain caused by inflammation of the spinal cord compounded by arthritis in the head, jaw, neck and spine, and by trigeminal neuralgia which causes pain in her mouth and face. Yet her will to fight back has increased in ratio to her illness.

Before she was confined to a wheelchair in 1978 she enrolled with the Open University to become an educational psychologist. It took seven years of study to qualify — often she got up at four in the morning to keep up with her schedule — and today she has children referred to her for remedial work.

'I have still got my skills in my head,' she says. 'This work began some years ago, when the child of one of my helpers was in trouble and needed help, and since then many disadvantaged and handicapped children have been sent for sessions with me. The fact that I conduct them from a wheelchair does not seem to matter.

'One thing that made me happy about getting my degree was that my father knew about it just before he died. There was a write-up in a newspaper about me with a photograph which I took to show him in hospital and he was absolutely thrilled. Sadly, my mother had died eleven months earlier but she knew I would do it.

'Nobody could have been more supportive than my parents and when Mummy died there was so much grief and emotion I had to get out of me — you can only cry so much and I had a child of fourteen to think of — that I decided I had to do something positive. I had to make use of the intense feelings within me, and so I began writing — it had to be about something beautiful, peaceful and about the good that is around us in the world.'

Wendy commenced a book on natural history and gardening, using a computer to get down the words and at that early stage illustrating it by hand. Halfway through she lost the use of her fingers and arms and had to change to painting with a brush held in her mouth just as she used a mouthstick to operate the computer keyboard.

'The book was my phoenix, something good and positive that came out of my grief,' she says. 'I had to try and be happy. It was a responsibility to my parents after all they had done for me.'

Wendy's gardening book is now complete after five years' work. She says that it does have a slant towards those with problems, the first chapter is about being handicapped but not necessarily physically, mentally or emotionally.

'You can be handicapped if you live in a bedsit and haven't got a garden and you want to grow an apple tree,' she declares. 'I have described things to make and do, adventurous things if you are hale and hearty and with money in the bank to buy materials, and — based on my own experience — there are things to do that don't need money and which are possible even if you are not well.

'When I was a child I used to write stories — imaginative rubbish! Dad would say something suitable and fatherly and then add, "Wendy, if you want to write anything that anyone will read you must write something about what you know." And that's what I have tried to do. I like writing. If you don't have anyone to tell things to you can tell them to your computer — and it doesn't interrupt you.'

At first Wendy found the technique of mouth-painting very difficult but she was so desperate to illustrate her book that she forced herself to carry on. One of her problems was that the mouthstick was too heavy and exhausting because of the arthritis in her jaw, and when she saw a painting by the well-known mouth-painter Charles Fowler she wrote to him for advice.

Apart from practical help, Charles told her about the Association of Mouth and Foot Painting Artists and suggested that when she had done six paintings she thought were reasonable she should submit them to the organisation. This she did at the beginning of 1989 and in June 1989 she was accepted as a student, the stipend she receives helping her to maintain her hard won independence.

This independence is symbolized by Wendy's house — The Beehive — in Herne Bay, Kent. Here she lives alone, with much of her equipment operated by mouth, though she might not look at it that way as she has the company of a high-spirited young Labrador bitch named Merryweather, her bees and her beautiful white doves. Because she is so disabled she requires the services of helpers, and has a rota of thirteen regulars and six who are standbys in case of emergency, such as when a regular might ring up and say, 'I've got 'flu so I dare not come near you.'

Wendy admits that it has been a fight to retain her right to lead a life of her own.

'I had to come off the Social Services because I am what they call too "cost dependent",' she says. 'It meant that by staying at home I needed more help than average and this was not fair to the others so I was told that I must go into residential care. I fought a great battle to remain in my own home, and from the Social Services' point of view I lost it because they were able to withdraw their assistance and continue saying that I should be in residential care. On the other hand I won in that I am still in my house and coping by employing my own carers.

'I receive no care help from the Social Services now and I pay my helpers myself — much easier since I joined the Mouth and Foot Painting Artists — and I shall stay in my own home as long as I possibly can.

'When I moved to this house, which is specially adapted for my electric wheelchair, I called it The Beehive because my parents had always called the homes we lived in by that name — from the B in Barber, my maiden name — and I carried on the tradition. Then people asked me, "Do you keep bees?" and I began to think "Why not?" I had always enjoyed bees and one day four years ago I said to Matthew, "I'm going to keep bees." And I waited. "Good!" he said and, unlike everyone else, he did not ask me how was I going to manage.'

Wendy managed by paying a boy, a tyro beekeeper, to follow her instructions and now has a double hive which she designed herself housing 50,000 bees at the bottom of her patio garden. Despite the 'Honey for sale' notice most of the honey produced is given away.

One of the problems of the paralysed is that they cannot brush away insects that land upon them, yet this does not trouble Wendy when she visits the hive.

'The bees know me,' she explains. 'They recognise the wheelchair and when they see it they say, "Here comes Wendy", and they sit on it which I find very pleasant. They never harm me though I do keep my mouth closed.'

In the centre of the patio garden is a dovecote around which flutter white doves and the occasional racing pigeon resting there until it is ready to continue its journey.

'I started with two pairs of doves', says Wendy. 'They had babies and their babies had babies and... anyway, there are eighteen now and I'm looking for homes. They are lovely to paint and like the bees they stay because they want to. I don't want to keep animals against their wish so I choose to have animals that could leave me if they want to.'

There is no likelihood of Merryweather the Labrador wanting to leave, she is utterly devoted to her mistress with whom she has lived since she was six weeks old. A year on Merryweather is being trained as an 'assistance dog' and already is useful when it comes to picking things up, but most of all she provides the rich bond of companionship between animal and human enjoyed by several other artists mentioned in this book.

Looking out on to the patio garden, with its flowers, bees and doves, is Wendy's studio. Here everything is designed for an artist confined to a wheelchair, and here she spends her happiest hours with the devoted Merryweather beside her. She paints mostly in water-colour, though she does sometimes use oils and coloured pencils.

'I paint in my head first,' she explains. 'I spend a long time building up the picture stroke by stroke in my mind. I need to know exactly where I am going with a picture because of the proximity of the paper to my nose when I actually paint. I need to hold a picture in my memory because executing it can be difficult — it takes me between two and three hundred hours to paint one.'

'I sometimes have to cope with two opposing wishes,' she says. 'My body wants me to stop painting and my brain wants me to keep on.'

Apart from pain-killing drugs, Wendy uses an electronic device based on acupuncture which sends an alternative current down the spine to alleviate the pain enough for her to be able to continue painting. Yet there is no hint of her difficulties in her clear bright paintings which usually depict animals and birds, the natural history subjects that she has always loved, as well as traditional subjects for greeting cards.

'I am now determined to become a full member of the Association,' Wendy says, 'and I'm so busy with my work that I don't have time to think about me — you survive that way. And I very, very much believe you should put more back into life than you take out, not for any commendable reason but self-preservation — you cannot be happy if you take out more than you are prepared to give.'

THE REVEREND
GLENN BARNETT

'I can never accept my disability.'

It was like being at the movies with my life story being projected on to my mind. Everything I had done wrong stood out from the rest. I remember in some sort of way calling out to God.'

Thus Glenn Barnett describes the moment when he lay drowning with a broken neck and an almost severed spinal cord. 'Those few moments were the most unusual I have ever spent. I knew I was going to drown yet I didn't panic. There was no fear, just a calmness as I inhaled the salt water.'

Glenn was born in 1947 in Port Lincoln, a typical country town in South Australia known as a major wheat port and the home of Australia's largest tuna fishing fleet. He describes himself as 'a typical country kid' of those days. He got into mischief, enjoyed roaming in the bush but best of all loved sport. At school he played football and cricket and became an athletics champion. In the 'sixties there was plenty of well paid work about and he could not wait to get out into the world and earn his own living. So at the age of fourteen he left High School to work in the spare parts department of a motor company.

The last day of November, 1962, was particularly hot and after work Glenn and a friend went to the local jetty to cool off in the sea. After they had been swimming for an hour it was time to go for their Friday night session of table tennis.

'Like typical lazy teenagers we thought it too far to walk back along the jetty,' Glenn says. 'Instead we would take a short cut by diving in and swimming to the shore. We usually did this but tonight we were closer to the shore than usual. We climbed on to the rail and I dived after singing out our usual "Break my neck".'

Those three words were a ghastly prophecy. Glenn dived twelve feet into two feet of water which being deceptively clear looked much deeper.

'I pile-dived myself into the sand at the bottom,' Glenn told the author. 'There was no pain, just a black flash. As I tried to stand up a strange tingling shot through my body and I found I could not move. I held my breath as long as I could and then began to breathe in water. Suddenly there was a lot of splashing and a boy called Graham Eastern dragged me to the shore. I thanked him but I doubt if he heard me. In fact I did not see him again for twenty-eight years when he returned to Port Lincoln on holiday with his wife. I took them out to dinner and was able to thank him properly — I have had a fantastic life and it would have been terrible to have lost it then.'

Luckily on the shore there was someone who knew what to do, packing sand round Glenn's neck to protect it until the ambulance arrived. His recollection of the events is hazy, people in a circle staring at him and then two nurses cutting away his swimming trunks in hospital and later being given liquid by means of a teapot-like object. The next day he was flown 150 miles to the Royal Adelaide Hospital where he had a tracheotomy and then an operation to graft a bone to support his broken neck.

Perhaps because he was only fifteen no one explained what had really happened to him and during the following weeks he lay in bed expecting to recover. It was only a nurse's accidental remark that broke the news to him that he would never walk again and, as he said, 'it felt as though my guts fell out'.

'There was no counselling in those days so I thought about it by myself over the weekend and I began to think that there were still things I could do in a wheelchair. Then I was transferred to the Spinal Injuries Unit at the Morris Hospital and put into a dining-room where I saw my fellow quadriplegics with their hands crippled up, and I realized I had not only lost my legs but also my arms and I felt devastated.'

At the end of a year it was decided that nothing more could be done for Glenn and he was sent home to his parents — something which filled him with dismay. In the hospital he felt secure among people disabled like himself but he was terrified of being stared at back in the world of the able-bodied.

At first he refused to go outside the house and then permitted himself to be wheeled on to the back verandah out of sight of the neighbours. It was his sister's sixteen-year-old boy friend (now Glenn's brother-in-law) who altered all this. He invited Glenn to a friend's house and when Glenn as usual refused he grabbed the wheelchair handles and raced with it down the drive and up the road with its occupant swearing and spitting at him in frustrated fury.

As it turned out this action was one of the best experiences of Glenn's life as it broke down the barrier he was erecting against the outside world. After that he lived as normal a life as possible with friends of his own age, going out to drive-in cinemas and parties and yelling at people out of car windows — 'those stupid things that teenagers do.'

One day a little boy who was being looked after by Mrs Barnett asked Glen to draw him a picture.

'I explained that I could not use my hands,' says Glenn. 'But next day I thought I would try with a pen in my mouth. I found I could draw lines fairly straight and asked mother to buy me some cheap water-colours and I began to splash around the paint. It developed slowly and I enjoyed it. In fact I felt very pleased with the results and it was only later that I realized how terrible they were. In such a situation you are encouraged with false praise when you start painting.'

In 1966 Glenn's mother had another child and because of a difficult pregnancy was unable to continue looking after him so he returned to the Morris Hospital as a long-termer.

Here he thought about life very deeply. His parents had been told that he could expect to live for about twenty-five years. How would he fill them? It seemed impossible to have a normal relationship with a member of the opposite sex, impossible to work and impossible to take part in sport which had been the most important aspect of his life.

The answer was provided by his fellow long-term patients — pleasure! This group decided that all that was left in life was pleasure which was obtained largely through alcohol.

'We got people to smuggle in booze for us,' said Glenn, 'and I often got drunk sitting in my wheelchair under the gum trees in the hospital grounds. I was taken to parties with the others and two or three times a week I would wake up with the night before a blank.'

Then, at the age of twenty, something very significant happened in his life. A new

54

gardener came to work in the grounds. He was a Pentecostal Christian and he urged Glenn to read the New Testament. Having been taught as a boy to respect his elders Glenn complied and spent the next few months studying the Gospels.

'The result was that I felt challenged personally,' he declares. 'A radical change came over me. My whole philosophy spun round and my need for pleasure was completely altered. I saw everything in a new way from then on, even things in nature, and I became a Christian.'

At that time Glenn had begun a deep friendship with one of the nurses at the hospital, Avril Saunders, who had grown up in the Methodist faith. As their relationship deepened they discussed the question of marriage but decided that it would be out of the question, not because of Glenn's disability but because it seemed financially impossible for them to live independently as man and wife.

Ever since his mother had bought him the box of water-colours Glenn had continued to paint even through his hangover days and, having seen a television programme on a mouth-painter, he got in touch with the Association of Mouth and Foot Painting Artists. He was so encouraged at the possibility of being able to make a living out of his art that he and Avril were married in 1971 in front of a congregation made up of 175 relations and friends. He was accepted as a full member of the Association in 1973 which meant that they were able to build a house in Adelaide Hills designed specially to suit a wheelchair.

Here Glenn settled down to a happy life with his wife and often painted up to eight hours a day.

'When I was at the Morris Hospital I wanted to go back to school,' he explains. 'So I was given tests to see if I had enough intelligence to study — and the result was that I was told to forget it. I was not smart enough and it would be a waste of time. But now I felt challenged by God to learn as much as I could and I began correspondence courses with Bible colleges. In 1976 I was accepted into the South Australian Bible College where alterations were actually made to the building to accommodate my wheelchair.'

After three years Glenn received his Diploma of Divinity with a distinction and was then offered a post as lecturer at the Uniting Church's Alcorn College, a lay training centre. While involved in this work he also studied to get a university degree.

In studying he was given no special advantages, no extra time to sit examinations even though he had to write his papers with a pen held in his mouth. In one three-hour exam he filled eighteen foolscap pages this way.

Having gone so far in lay work Glenn now felt inspired to go further. From 1981 to 1983 he studied at Trinity College, Brisbane, and was ordained as a Minister of the Uniting Church in 1984. His first parochial work was at Bundaberg in the heart of Queensland's cane and cattle country.

In an interview on his work there, Glenn told a journalist, 'I loved parish ministry and the wheelchair presented almost no difficulties despite most Queensland houses being high-set. I could get into most of them to visit people and at those I couldn't the people were happy to come into the garden for a chat. I've been able to take weddings and funerals, even in the mud at the graveside.'

His ministry was very much a team effort with Avril acting as his chauffeur, sounding board and critic.

After Bundaberg Glenn moved to South Australia to continue his pastoral work in Port Broughton. Apart from the usual role of a minister he made a point of speaking to schools and numerous community groups on disablement at which he would give demonstrations of his painting technique.

Sadly in 1989 Glenn received a severe jolt in a car in which he was travelling which affected his neck so that, despite an operation, his condition deteriorated and it became necessary for him to give up church work at the beginning of 1991. For his 'retirement' he and Avril bought a house in his home town of Port Lincoln, and here Glenn continues to paint though the amount of time he can spend on it at one time is reduced to four hours a day.

This, however, has not in any way dampened his enthusiasm for art; on the contrary he is possibly more enthusiastic than ever and he is now two-thirds of the way through a Master of Arts degree.

'I find painting totally fulfilling,' he declares. 'And I see it as something more than just pictures because I believe art stimulates peoples' thoughts about reality. I am often told that I must be at peace with myself because my work demonstrates peace, and I think that's true.

'I paint mainly landscapes, travelling all over Australia with Avril to get subjects, and camping out in the heart of the bush. My greatest love is the Flinders Ranges — they are magnificent with very splendid colours and I keep going back to them.'

In talking to Glenn one finds that while the conversation may be serious it never strays far from humour. A discussion on philosophy might suddenly turn into an anecdote on how at his sister's wedding something went wrong with the portable plumbing required through his disability with the result that as his wheelchair progressed down the church it left a trickle the length of the aisle — or how on his first day at a parish in Queensland the lifting device to help him out of the car broke and sent him sprawling full length at the feet of the minister he was going to work with.

Back on the philosophical side he says, 'I am one of those strange people who can never accept my disability. To me it is silly to say I accept it — of course I would rather be able to walk! You adjust to rather than accept disability, and I have managed to do this through my art work and as a Christian. Avril and I have had a happy and amazing life together and we could not have done this without me being able to earn my living as an artist.'

JOHN BUNCE

'Painting by numbers'

A person's life can be altered in a single second so that for however many more years he or she may live nothing will ever be the same again. So it was for twenty-year-old John Bunce when in 1952 he was doing his National Service in the British Army's catering corps in Germany, work he enjoyed so much he had resolved to train to be a chef when he was demobbed.

One evening in his billet after coming off duty, he stood by his bed and reached up to replace a book on a high shelf and he somehow missed his footing. As he felt himself fall he twisted so that he would land on his bed, and as he did so a blinding pain shot through his head. What he had not known was that a metal toolbox had been pushed under the bed. That was what his head had struck.

Lying as he had fallen he found it impossible to move and that he could speak no louder than a whisper. An inconsequential thought flashed through his brain: 'Now I shall get out of the C.O.'s inspection tomorrow.'

His second thought was that it might be 'the end of the line', as he put it. As a boy he had sung in a church choir, and now thought of the faith he had been taught returned to him. In his almost inaudible voice he asked his fellow soldiers who stood shocked around the bed to repeat the Lord's Prayer with him.

'It was remarkable how much it helped me at that moment,' recalls John who for the last few years has been a member of the Christadelphian Church.

When John arrived in a military hospital he could not speak at all, and it was found that he had broken his fifth vertebra with the result that he was paralysed from the neck down. From Germany he was taken to the Stoke Mandeville Hospital's special injury unit where he was subjected to intensive physiotherapy. His doctors were particularly interested in him because at the time he had the highest lesion of the vertebra they had seen.

With treatment John's voice returned and also enough movement in one arm to be able to pilot an electric wheelchair by means of a special 'joystick', but after two years it was realized there could be no further improvement and the young man was sent home to his parents.

While at the hospital John remembers he was 'bored out of his mind' and that he could not sit like some of the others making 'baskets and fluffy dolls'. In order to occupy him with something that was not beyond his very limited capability a member of staff suggested he might like to try 'painting by numbers' by means of a brush held in his mouth.

The first attempt was not inspiring but looking back on it John thinks that everything started from there.

Then, when John went home to his parents, the idea of occupying himself by means of a pencil held in his mouth presented itself again.

'To pass the time while I lay in bed I used to read those little comic war books, and with a pencil I copied some of the pictures — a face or a tank — in the margin,' he recalls. 'I really enjoyed this, especially when my mother was out and I was left alone in the house and had to fill in time as best I could.'

From the margins of comics John progressed to sketching on scrap paper, much to the surprise of a welfare official who urged John to enter a pencil sketch in an art competition. When it was announced that John Bunce was the winner it gave him the encouragement he needed to take his art further, especially as the judges had had no idea that the man responsible for the winning entry was disabled. At that time John's problem with his work was that for some reason he was nervous of colour and when he made his first attempt with water-colour his worst fears were confirmed. Propped up in bed, he found that the paint ran down the paper quicker than he could control it with his brush, and soon the coverlet was damp and tinted with pale colours. Yet when the brushes were put away and the paintbox closed John knew that he wanted to try again.

Soon painting became John's only escape from the grimmer realities of life.

'I had split up with my wife — she had found someone else as so often happens when a husband or wife becomes disabled,' he says, 'And while I was back in hospital for a spell I learned that my father was suffering from cancer. What I wanted most was to be close to where my Dad was. The only way I could do this was to go into a Cheshire Home in Wolverhampton which being only eight miles away enabled me to visit him frequently.'

At one time or another several members of the Mouth and Foot Painting Artists Association have stayed in Cheshire Homes which were the inspiration of Group Captain Leonard Cheshire VC OM, who got the idea of founding such an establishment after he had taken a serviceman who was dying of cancer into his own home. His aim was to make them as 'un-institutional' as possible, to be places of shelter and spiritual encouragement. The first of these homes was Le Court in Hampshire where the well-known mouth artist Albert Baker lived for a long time. Today there are many Cheshire Homes in Britain and abroad and they are open for any disabled person to apply for residence without any reference to race or religion.

'I would recommend this type of establishment to anyone with a serious disability,' says John. 'It doesn't restrict you. You are not a prisoner within your own four walls. Of course it is lovely to be at home, it's private and you have your relatives round you, but it doesn't give you very much scope. At a Cheshire Home, whether you are trying to do artwork or writing or whatever, you get a fair amount of criticism and encouragement from the staff and visitors.'

In fact John found that Le Court suited him so well that he stayed there for seven years and then transferred to the Greenacres Cheshire Home in Sutton Coldfield where he lives today.

Meanwhile his interest in drawing and painting persisted and in 1974 it was suggested that he should contact the Association of Mouth and Foot Painting Artists, an organisation he had never heard of until then. After some of his paintings were evaluated he became a student and then a member eleven years later. The period of learning was very useful to John who, he admits, had never been taught anything about art. He says the most important thing he learned was to be critical of his own work to the point when he would scrap a painting if he felt it did not come up to standard.

John's work has won him a number of prizes. Recently he achieved the highest award in the DHSS national art competition and also claimed the top awards for water-colours and oils in the independent regional competition. In these competitions paintings are considered without the judges knowing the names of the artists responsible for them.

Health permitting John works every day in a room at Greenacres whose glass walls overlook a garden and which makes a perfect studio. He works at an easel which he designed himself. Electric motors tilt the board and raise it up and down but what is so special about it is that John can control it with a mouthstick which has a magnet mounted on the end. A touch of the magnet on one of the squares set in a panel is enough to activate the mechanism.

Another of his innovations is a light metal frame which clamps on to the arms of his wheelchair and holds his camera at eye level. Photography is useful to him when he wants to capture a scene for a future painting when out in the countryside and composition is achieved by manoeuvring his electric wheelchair.

John is catholic in his choice of subjects and the materials he uses which include coloured inks, oils and water-colours.

'I enjoy painting whatever I am painting at the time,' he says. 'I have no preference at all. I like painting a woodland scene as much as a house, a seascape as much as a bowl of flowers.'

An intriguing aspect of John's work is his secret 'signature'; in every picture he incorporates a minute rabbit which may be no more than a shape caused by shadow or a rabbit-shaped patch of sky seen through foliage. Children who come to watch him work regard his pictures as puzzles as they seek the hidden bunny.

Apart from giving art lessons to both children and adults John does a lot of work for charitable causes through demonstrations of his mouth-painting technique at church fêtes and similar gatherings, and he is also invited to schools.

He says, 'Usually I go for a whole morning or afternoon but sometimes when it is a large school I go for a whole day. To win the pupils' interest I do an on-the-spot portrait of whoever has a birthday that day, or whose birthday is closest. I tell them about being disabled and about my work so that I try to get across to them that if a person is in a wheelchair he or she is approachable.

'Like everyone I do have some regrets, one being that I did not meet Erich Stegmann who founded the Association and did so much to help people like me. Although you can work on your own as a disabled artist, the Association gives you something to aim for and it enables you to meet other artists who are in your situation.'

FLORENCE BUNN

'The best pain-killer I know.'

You will not find this a story of triumph in the face of adversity,' Florence Bunn told the author. 'It is a love story.' And as she continued it became obvious what she meant.

Memories of her young days are very happy ones. Her father was an artistic craftsman of many talents, one of which was sign-writing the names of firms on glass doors in gold leaf. He was so proficient that he could put the lettering on backwards as was required without the help of a mirror which was the usual method employed. Florence remembers what a treat it was to be allowed to watch him, holding back any coughs or sneezes because gold leaf is so light the slightest movement of the air could carry it away.

Florence, who had been born in West Hartlepool in 1937, enjoyed being a schoolgirl and this fostered the ambition to become a teacher. To this end she later went to St Hilda's College in Durham where she specialized in mathematics. In 1955 this was still regarded as an unusual subject for a woman to undertake and she had to attend a male college for lectures.

When she had completed her course Florence returned home to teach in a girls' secondary school which was amalgamated with a boys' school in the early 'sixties.

'I stayed at the school for nine years,' Florence says. 'I found time to be a youth leader three nights a week and I became involved in the Church Young Fellowship as well. I was a lucky young woman enjoying amateur dramatics, playing tennis and badminton — occasionally with the man who was to become my husband. Who says that game-love means you've lost!'

This man was Geoff Bunn and he had known Florence from their babyhood.

'Our parents who lived in the same street were friends before we were born,' explains Geoff. 'And we were born within weeks of each other. We still have a photograph of us both taken at the age of eighteen months. Our families went on holiday together and if the war had not come along they would have emigrated to Canada together. Today I still find it strange that Florence can tell me anecdotes about my relatives that I have never heard before.

'During the war my father moved the family to Blackpool — he still had memories of West Hartlepool being bombarded in the First World War when he was a young apprentice — but we used to go back for holidays and my highlight of the week was to sit on the same settee as Florence, eating fish and chips and then singing songs round the piano — as we still do.'

This way Geoff and Florence remained in contact until she went to college and he served in the navy when they lost touch for ten years.

'In 1965 a cousin of mine invited me to a wedding in Hartlepool,' says Geoff. 'I went — and found that the bridesmaid was Florence. This time there was no question of us losing contact.'

It was about this time that Florence found that minor things were going wrong with her health. Once her tongue became numb and her fingers tingled strangely but after a few days these odd symptoms disappeared. Her doctor told her that as the educational system was going through massive changes at the time she was finding it stressful and all she needed was a few days' rest.

'I was young and enthusiastic and I just thought my body was warning me to slow down a bit,' says Florence. 'In July 1966 Geoff and I were married. I continued teaching for another couple of years until my first son was born. Our second son was born in 1971 and I had a hint that all was not well during the pregnancy. Soon afterwards multiple sclerosis was diagnosed.

'One of the unfortunate spin-offs of early MS is that one looks drunk because of the loss of balance and whereas a helpful hand would be nice the reality is a cold shoulder,' she says. 'I began to use elbow crutches but I found housework and looking after two active toddlers becoming more and more difficult so I went back to education as a home tutor and was able to pay for help in the house.

'Home tutors are a band of people who take on the education of youngsters who — usually through illness — have been away from school and need special help to catch up. I found I had to teach everything and they were four happy years because I really felt I was doing something worthwhile. One of my early pupils was a girl with a spinal problem and I was so pleased when the other day she brought round her daughter to meet me.

'At home we began using labour-saving gadgets that were almost ahead of my time. A washing-machine, dishwasher, foodmixer and so on eased the problems of two small boys and my husband who still prefers homecooking.'

By 1977 a new gadget had to be introduced — an electric wheelchair but due to the inexorable progress of the disease Florence began to lose the use of her hands with the result that she was unable to control the chair. One day the postman brought her green employment card from the Education Office.

'Dear Geoff didn't tell me about it at first and when I did find out it was a psychological blow — I was unemployable,' Florence recalls. 'I started going to a day care centre one day a week and was very unhappy for a very long time. It was nobody's fault but I could not get used to the idea of being disabled, of not even being able to feed myself.

'Eventually a young instructor anxious to find something that would fill in my time suggested drawing by mouth. I remember how hard he searched the building for a suitable table and pencil-holder for me to use. I felt silly but he had tried so hard the least I could do was try as well.'

As Florence became proficient in using mouth-held pencils and brushes she wondered how she could put her new-found interest to practical use. In 1983 she hit on the idea of designing decorative stationery and having it printed to sell at a craft fair. Soon afterwards she received a letter from the Association of Mouth and Foot Painting Artists asking her if she would send in some examples of her work. Apparently a reporter covering the fair had described the stationery produced by Florence — the headline read 'The Art of Florence' — and a cutting of the story reached the Association in London.

When there was no immediate response Florence sent in more of her work to prove that her first consignment was not 'a flash in the pan'. Soon afterwards she was offered a studentship.

'An immediate benefit was that I began to believe more in myself,' Florence says. 'We think we don't constantly want admiration yet underneath we do. What I mean is that we want to be accepted, we want someone to notice us. And the important thing about becoming a student is that you have someone backing you. And what I did not realize was how many fellow mouth and foot painting students there were in the world.

'It was like joining a great big family that you kept in touch with through our international magazine. And then there were the exhibitions of members' work. I remember going down to London to a big exhibition in the Royal Festival Hall and seeing the paintings there I realized how much harder I needed to work. I saw other disabled artists at work and they inspired me because they showed me just what could be done. Then — and at the other exhibitions I have been invited to since — I come away saying to myself, "If I try harder I might just manage that."

'When we got back to our home in Blackpool Geoff built me an easel with a board powered by a little electric motor so that it moves up and down and gives me much more scope. I also had to find a better way of moving in front of the easel. I had begun sitting in an armchair but I could not move back to see what I had done.' This problem was finally solved by a specially adapted electric wheelchair which she can control by movement of her chin on a suitably shaped control bar.

Florence worked on with a determination to become a full member. At first she had produced postcard-sized pictures but the motorized easel Geoff had made increased her scope. She settled on gouache as her medium because she liked its strong colours. Her favourite subject was — and still is — still life studies of flowers which Geoff picks for her in the garden of their home.

Able-bodied artists will agree that painting is not an easy occupation. It requires continual concentration both mental and physical and the need to remain more or less in one position in front of an easel for long periods. How much more difficult for a disabled person like Florence with the added difficulties of only having movement from the base of her neck up and being in frequent pain.

'Because I want to remain clear-headed through the day for the sake of my family as well as for the sake of my work I do not take any pain-killers though at night I do have to take something to make me sleep,' she explains. 'Painting takes my mind off the discomfort. It's the best pain-killer I know and there are no side effects.'

Florence's hard work paid off. She became a full member of the Association in March 1988.

Thanks to the financial security this meant Geoff was able to give up his job with British Telecom in order to look after Florence full-time though she still jealously guards what little independence is left to her.

'I like to paint by myself as much as possible,' she says. 'Of course Geoff has to put the paints out for me but when that is done I am left alone to get on with it. I could not feel I was doing it by myself if someone was helping me too much.'

Apart from her paintings which are sent to the Association Florence likes to experiment in other fields. She paints on porcelain which Geoff fires for her in her own kiln. Some of the vases she showed the author were quite remarkable with abstract decoration composed of spattered paint and gilded.

'To get the effect I mixed the paint with milk and blew it on with a straw,' she laughed. 'The gold I put on with a brush. I like that part — perhaps it reminds me of watching my father work with gold. With ceramics there is the thought that unless they get broken my work is there forever.'

Another aspect of becoming a full member of the Association that delighted Florence was that it gave her the sense of belonging to a world-wide family. After it was announced in the Association's journal that she had been accepted as a member she received a letter from India written by a disabled artist there who had become a member on the same day and an interesting and amusing correspondence has continued ever since. A similar letter arrived from Canada and there are opportunities for her to meet her fellow painters on the occasions when conferences are arranged.

'It has given life a whole new meaning,' she says, 'though of course I still have my off times. If I get gloomy Geoff reminds me of the pluses in my life by bringing out something I did ages ago.

'"Can you remember this?" he asks. "You liked it at the time. What do you think of it now?"

'"Dreadful!" I reply and this reminder of the progress I have made does me good.

'The problem with MS is that it is progressive and we have had to adapt and adapt and adapt again as my condition has worsened. People thought that changing the geography of our bathroom was some weird hobby we had because we did it so often! The disease affects the central nervous system which controls movement though it is not the nerves themselves that are affected but the sheaths covering them. No one has any idea why one is afflicted by it and as yet there is no cure.

'There is always a bit of a cloud over you that it will get worse and you wonder if you will be able to take it. I cannot deny pain exists in plenty and would like to comfort those who can't cope. Incurable progressive conditions are a burden which can crush the spirit but a wise doctor is beyond price. It is all too tempting to think that there is nothing he can do. That isn't true. Research is going on all the time but I have been guided away from fashionable "cures" and instead been given gentle sustained encouragement while the scientists get to the root of the problem.

'I have had MS for twenty years now, but I count myself lucky that I have two caring sons one of whom is an art-student, a husband who has stood by me — and my painting.

'Geoff is extremely calm — and funny. He often makes jokes about my disability. They are never in bad taste, they just make me laugh. When straightening out my cushions he will say, "One lump or two." And I remember after a particularly nice meal we had in a hotel — having to be fed in public does not deter me — I waxed philosophical and observed that life is full of peaks and troughs. Geoff, looking at my empty plate asked if this was a peak or a trough.

'Geoff wants to keep me smiling and — Boy! — do I want to impress him!'

JOHN BUTLER

A whole new life

Frederick John Butler was named after his father who had been named after John's grandfather, but apart from this very little of his father's influence remains with him.

'I have very few memories of my early childhood,' says John, 'But across the road from where we lived on the south side of Brisbane there was a park and I do have a recollection of flying a kite there. All I remember of my father was going to a soccer match with him and to a roller skating rink where I had skates put on my feet. My mother and father separated when I was four and so he is a stranger for whom I have no feelings.'

John, who was born in 1940, speaks with glowing admiration of his mother's battle to keep a home going for him and his two younger brothers after the family was left without financial assistance.

'She was a petite lady with blonde hair and blue eyes and a wonderful sense of fun,' he recalls. 'She was always ready to laugh at herself and had the wonderful ability to find humour in some of the most serious situations. In those days there was very little support for the single parent. I remember my mother coming home and telling her sister how she had been told by the police that if she could locate her husband, who had vanished in Sydney, they would force him to pay the maintenance due to her, but if she could not give them his address there was nothing they could do.'

After this she resigned herself to the task of rearing her boys alone. She had been a machinist in a factory and had a gift for sewing, and it was by sewing that she supported the family though John remembers there were times when she actually went without food herself in order that the three growing boys should not be hungry.

'For a while we lived with my grandmother and I remember that was a happy period of my life,' he says. 'Then a housing scheme was started to provide accommodation for families in the lower socio-economic group but in order to get into it we had to spend eighteen months in a halfway house which in reality was an old army barracks where we shared two rooms at the end of a long hut. Yet, although we were dreadfully poor, Mother never allowed herself or her sons to be seen that way.

'She was always neat in her dress and she made clothes for us — even our slippers out of felt — so that we always looked good.'

After the period in the barracks the family was able to move to the housing scheme in an outer suburb of Brisbane which, being seven miles from the city centre, seemed 'as far away as Mars' to the boys.

John was now ten and apart from attending the local primary school he went to

Sunday School which, because of its proximity to their house, the boys reached by climbing over the back fence. John became what is termed a 'born again' Christian, and today he declares, 'My faith in God has been a life preserver for me. I do not know how I would have coped without my faith.'

The other thing that was to help him cope in the dark days that lay ahead was a philosophy that his mother had instilled into him and his brothers.

'She taught us that the world does not owe us a living and that unless we get off our backsides and help ourselves no one else will.'

During his teenage years John became a leader of a church youth club, working with boys who had similar backgrounds to his own. In his second year at secondary school he passed his Grade 10 exams and though he would have liked to continue his education it was financially necessary for him to leave school. His mother told him he could have 'two weeks holiday and nine months to find work'.

It did not take nine months. After his two-week break John dressed in his best clothes and walked the streets of Brisbane in search of a job. He had no clear idea of what he wanted to do until one day he found himself passing the premises of a jewellery business. Pressing his nose against the window he saw rows of watchmakers bent over their benches and, intrigued by what they were doing, he approached the manager who said that while there was no vacancy for an apprentice watchmaker, there was one in the jewellery manufacturing department. He took the boy upstairs to some dingy rooms where half a dozen men were sitting over benches under bright lights.

'Looking over their shoulders I saw they were taking lengths of gold and using various devices to change its shape,' John remembers. 'They filed and soldered and when I saw the finished work I was absolutely fascinated by the way the metal was transformed into things of beauty.'

John took the job and the art of making jewellery fired him with ambition. He set up a workbench in his home so that at night he could practice what he was learning through the day at work and college. In 1966, when he completed his five-year apprenticeship, he was named Apprentice of the Year — to the delight of his mother who had given him great support.

Two years later he married his wife Kay and in 1972 the couple started their own jewellery business in the foyer of a big insurance company building in Brisbane's business area. John specialized in designing and making exclusive jewellery pieces with emeralds, rubies and diamonds, and the following year he came first in the men's section of the Australian Jewellery Design Award and second in another category. All was going well and the happiness of the young couple was increased by the arrival of their first son Scott.

In 1976 John, who was still a youth leader and played guitar with a Christian band, took part in a boys' camp where he was infected by a mysterious virus. This resulted in a very distressing condition now thought to have been severe rheumatoid arthritis which is defined as a 'chronic progressive general disease of uncertain origin leading to inflammatory changes in the tissues, especially the joints.'

In John's case his knees and feet were so badly affected he could hardly walk while his fingers became so swollen that it was impossible for him to continue his delicate jewellery work.

'We struggled on and friends in the trade were wonderful but eventually we had to close the business,' he says. 'I was filled with depression, and I remember one day as we were closing down we took the lift to the fifth floor which was a roof car park. I could walk only with great difficulty and as I neared the edge of the building it came into my mind that if I threw myself over the railing it would be the end of

65

the pain and depression overwhelming me. The financial difficulties that were haunting us would be over for Kay as she would collect insurance and, being a beautiful woman, she would have the opportunity to marry again and start a new life instead of having to look after a cripple.'

John looked at the rail and the drop beyond which seemed an answer to all problems but something held him back . . .

'It seems almost farcical today,' he says. 'But that is how I felt at that moment. If I had gone over the rail I would have missed so much that is good in life, and I mention this because it just might be of help to someone else.'

By Easter 1977 John and Kay had wound up their business and in considerable debt moved to Toowoomba in Queensland.

'The business firms we owed money to, especially our diamond merchant in Sydney, were marvellous and were prepared to wait for payment,' says John. 'There was a business opportunity in Toowoomba because, although being Australia's largest provincial city, there was no manufacturing jeweller there. My condition had improved enough for me to work four hours a day doing jewellery repairs in a small room and this way I managed to clear all the debts that had accumulated because of my ill health.'

The next year daughter Leah was born, the second of the Butlers' four children, and at last it seemed that John was recovering from his illness. With renewed energy he started to work twelve hours a day six days a week in order to regain his former standard of living. The result was that he had a relapse and became totally disabled.

He told the author, 'I became bed-ridden, unable to move and in extreme pain — even the pressure of a flannel on my skin made me scream in agony. I mention this, not because I want you to feel sorry for me but so you will understand the devotion of my wife who had to nurse me in that condition day after day after day. She still has to feed me three times daily, attend to my physical needs, scratch me if I have an itch, bring a drink if I need it . . . and yet she manages to do it all with good humour and somehow makes *me* feel I am a wonderful person. Through it all we have become very close and surprisingly have had an awful lot of laughs.'

In March 1983 John came into contact with two people who were to be instrumental in changing his life. At that time all he could do was lie in bed and, being unable to hold a book, spend his hours watching daytime television. He was visited by a 'blue nurse' — the term for a district nurse — who bathed him, and then by an occupational therapist named Betty McEwan. The blue nurse told him how she had met a disabled lady in New South Wales named Margaret Greig who did wonderful paintings with a brush held in her mouth and had he ever thought of trying that.

'I replied that I had never ever considered it,' says John, 'though now I can't understand why as when I was working I used to make drawings of jewellery and towards the end of my career as a jeweller I painted my designs in water-colour. I spoke to Betty McEwan about the idea and she found out about the organisation of disabled painters to which Margaret Greig belonged.'

'My wife bought my first set of paints and brushes and having been propped up, I began my first painting — a copy of a photograph of the Sahara Desert in an old *National Geographic* magazine. We still have it because Kay refuses to throw it away, saying we should keep it so that if we ever meet someone else disabled who needs encouragement with their painting they can see the Sahara picture and compare it with what I can do now to realize how it is possible to improve.

'Once I got interested in painting, I painted and I painted and I painted until I had five pictures I felt were good enough to submit to the Association of Mouth and Foot Painting Artists in Sydney.'

John's enthusiasm changed to disappointment as weeks and then months passed without even an acknowledgement. Finally he wrote and got an immediate reply explaining that there had been a fire in the office that had destroyed all records including his address. Would he kindly submit some more paintings? John complied with the result that in 1985 he was enrolled as a student and visited by Bruce Peardon who explained what the Association expected of him and was very supportive.

In order to improve his work John used his stipend to buy tutorial art books and videos which were useful as it was too difficult for him to attend local art classes. In 1988 it was considered that his painting had reached a high enough standard for him to have a one-man exhibition which was mounted in July, the middle of the Australian winter. Despite the fact that it was blowing a gale and the temperature was down to five degrees when it opened a hundred and fifty people attended, and a thousand dollars was raised to buy art materials for the Kath Dixon Centre, a community-funded project which runs a kindergarten and provides toys and books for disabled children.

'In 1989 I was staying with Bruce Peardon in his home on the coast when a telephone call came from Sydney to say that my work had reached the standard required for me to become a full member,' says John. 'It meant a whole new life for me. I no longer needed to be dependent on Social Security and it is a wonderful achievement to be able to say that you are making your own way. At last I was able to have my own studio with beautiful lighting from skylights, and a computer to deal with my correspondence. I also have a marvellous motorized easel, made by engineering students of the local university, which raises and lowers my canvas and moves it left or right as I require.

'Art has taken over most of my life. My family who once thought whatever I did was wonderful, are now more discerning — in fact they are my best critics. When I am not working in my studio I lie down to rest and watch tutorial art videos or sketch preliminary designs on a special easel which fits on the bed. From time to time I give demonstrations of mouth-painting and often members of the public say, "I have been buying these cards for years — it's so nice to meet someone who actually paints them."

'When I go to a school for disabled children they watch me and some are even learning to paint as a result, not that I care whether or not they want to paint — what concerns me is that they explore the limits of their capabilities and then push beyond them so that they can be fulfilled in their own right and in their own lives.'

STEVEN CHAMBERS

Left Stranded

Arthrogypoesis is the name of the rare and mysterious condition which afflicted Steven Chambers. He believes that there are only twenty others who share his ailment in Great Britain. The cause of arthrogypoesis is not known but its effect upon Steven was that he was born with his arms complete in every way except one — they were without muscles. The condition was further complicated by the painful stiffening of the leg joints. At the Great Ormond Hospital for Sick Children his mother and father were told that it was most unlikely that he would ever walk.

It was a pronouncement that Steven's mother refused to accept. During the periods he was out of hospital she continuously massaged his legs and made him do exercises to strengthen his lower limbs though nothing could be done for his arms which hung uselessly at his sides. It was then that she showed the determination which has been a key factor in her son's life.

'She used to take me into the garden and prop me up on my feet against a wall,' says Steven as though explaining a humorous episode. 'Then she would leave me so that I was stranded there. This used to happen every day until I got so fed up with it that I began to take steps and from then on I actually started walking. The fact that I can walk about today is due to willpower and my Mum!'

For a while the child had to wear callipers and later Steven underwent an operation to have a weak knee joint 'fused' into a permanent position in order to bear his weight and there is the possibility that he might require a similar operation on his other knee later on.

Until he was sixteen Steven was in and out of hospital but this did not hamper his education.

'I went to an ordinary school,' he explains, 'and there I was accepted as an ordinary person. I was never treated as though I was disabled. I think that this was due to the attitude my mother and father instilled in me — to always carry on as though I was not handicapped. Of course there were a lot of things I could not do and I had to accept that and make the best of what I could do.'

When Steven was unable to attend school his teachers took it in turns to visit him in hospital with his lessons so he would not be behind when he returned to class. They also went to his home when he had exams coming after he broke his leg. This came about when his friends announced they were going into the woods near his home in Denham, Middlesex. His father warned him not to go with them, saying it would be dangerous because the ground was full of holes covered by long grass. But Steven loved the outdoors and the thought of his friends having fun among the trees was too much for the boy. As soon as he could get out of sight of his family he joined them in the woods and proved the truth of his father's words by tripping over and breaking his leg.

From the beginning Steven used his mouth to hold a pencil — 'Not difficult because I had never known anything different.' What did frustrate him was that often he could not get the effects with it that he wanted.

'I had a very short temper as a child,' he admits. 'Sometimes I would throw down the pen in a rage, and my mother would make me carry on until I could do what I set out to. Once I wanted to cut some paper with a pair of scissors but it seemed an impossible task. "You just sit until you work out a way to do it," my mother said and she left me alone in the room. Somehow or other I finally managed to hold one of the scissors' handles in my mouth and work the blades along the paper which lay flat on the table. Since then I have always managed to cut my own paper.'

Perhaps because his grandfather was an artist Steven enjoyed art classes while at school though at the time he had no ambition to become a professional painter. When he left school at the age of eighteen he hoped to get employment on computers in the Martin Baker ejection seat company where his father was a designer but to his intense disappointment this did not materialize.

'So I went to art college for something to do,' he says. 'There was a nurse who took an interest in me and my work, and in 1980 she suggested that I got in touch with the Association of Mouth and Foot Painting Artists. I sent in some of my work and two weeks later I was offered a studentship.'

Since then he has continued to live with his family and develop his art work. So far the two things of which he is most proud is that his work was shown in a Canadian exhibition and a rabbit character which he painted for children was well received in Japan.

To begin with Steven painted in oils but like some other mouth painters he found these too difficult and now he uses water-colours.

'It is so much easier to clean a brush by rinsing it in a jar of water than having to clean oil from the bristles with turps,' he says. What frustrates him with artwork sometimes is not the technique of painting but the question of inspiration. On some occasions he will get his art materials out only to find that after an hour he puts them away without a line being drawn. At other times the reverse is true. When the creative urge is upon him he paints right through the night and is surprised when day breaks. He particularly likes drawing animals and apart from his straightforward work he loves to let his imagination run wild.

Steven's penchant for fantasy finds reign as a make-up artist. For many years his brother has been an addict of the game 'Dungeons and Dragons' in which each player takes on the role of a character in an amazingly complicated fantasy world such as one might find in the works of J. R. R. Tolkien. Since boyhood he played this game with a group of friends and now that they have grown up they have taken the game further and actually act it out. Each member of the group takes it in turn to be 'dungeon master' and map out the nature of the forthcoming game and then the players, fully costumed and equipped as the characters they portray, take to the woods. The rules are very strict; for example they cannot take modern food with them but must survive on fruit and home-baked bread. A flask of water is the only drink allowed.

Not only do they dress like characters in these role plays but they make-up like them — no doubt to the surprise of unsuspecting visitors to the woodland! Here Steven's skill comes into use making up the players as elves, halflings, dwarves and so on. He also designs their costumes.

On top of this Steven works on the most unusual 'canvas' of any mouth-painter

— the bodies of cars. Fascinated by cars himself, he is in great demand by enthusiasts whose hobby is the customizing of VW Beetles to decorate them with his designs. Although he cannot drive his interest in cars extends to making the most exquisite and detailed models which are then lovingly painted. At first thought it seems impossible that such miniatures could be the work of a man who has no other means of assembling them than with his mouth yet Steven uses his lips to hold the tiny pieces and to use the special glue to bond them together. He remarks cheerfully that the only thing he has to watch is that 'I don't swallow the bits.'

For someone who has no use in his arms and who was once thought to be incapable of walking, Steven has a wide range of interests which includes his unusual pets such as the Australian lizards who grew so big they had to be finally domiciled in the conservatory. These days his animal friends consist of a parrot, two gerbils, a dog which is a cross between a Labrador and an Alsatian, and a delightful chinchilla who loves to perch on his shoulder. When one touches her it becomes obvious why the beautifully soft grey chinchilla fur was so prized by furriers.

Next to painting Steven's favourite occupation is night fishing.

'I fish with my brother in a local lake,' he says. 'It is surrounded by woodland and the wildlife is marvellous. We go there in the evening and walk about the shore and then settle down for fishing at about 9 o'clock. What I love about it is the peace. And as far as the actual fishing is concerned I can do everything except take the fish off the hook. I use a very light rod which is well balanced and my father made a nylon mouthpiece which enables me to hold it.'

When the author visited Steven it was just three weeks after his marriage. His wife Jo, who enthusiastically shares his many interests, is a children's nanny and had only known Steven six weeks when they began discussing the question of marriage.

'We talked it over one weekend and decided that this was what we both wanted,' Steven recalls. 'I went home and announced that I was going to be married and my family said "Fine!" and by Tuesday night I had made arrangements with the church, booked a hall for the reception, bought the rings and got myself a new suit. And the wedding was a fantastic family affair.'

Despite arthrogypoesis Steven Chambers has built up a full life for himself and now there remains only one goal. 'My ambition,' he says, 'is to become a full member of the Association.'

JOY CLARKE

'You have to love the things you paint.'

Disabled artists often gain inspiration for their work from things they loved in the days when they were fit and mobile — Paul Driver with marine scenes, Derrick Vandek with the outdoors — and Joy Clarke with flowers. Her studies of delicate and detailed flower arrangements are painted with a love for growing things that goes back to the days when young Joy worked in garden nursery.

It was not an occupation that she had planned; indeed she had started an A-level course at school when circumstances forced her to give up her studies and take a job — she chose horticulture because of her interest in plants — in order to keep her mother's home going.

During Joy's childhood in Parkestone, Dorset, her mother suffered from a very rare neurological disease known as the Charcot-Marie Tooth Syndrome.

Despite the effect of her mother's illness on Joy and her brother, she says that she loved living in Dorset and had a good childhood.

'Then, when I was sixteen, I realized that there was something not quite right with me,' she says. 'I was still at school and I found that I could not do things in the gym that once came easily. After a school medical I was sent to an orthopaedic surgeon because my feet were painful and had become an awful shape.'

Although her mother's illness had begun with her feet, it did not occur to her that the Charcot-Marie Tooth Syndrome could be hereditary. Nor did her mother want to believe that she had passed on such a serious complaint to her daughter.

'Having suffered so much herself, she could not accept the fact that there was anything really wrong with me,' Joy explains. 'She wanted to ignore it, and I think she was quite firm if not rude to the surgeon who wanted to do something about my feet and the matter was dropped.'

Soon after this Joy had to get to work because her mother's condition worsened and she was without the support of a husband. For a year the girl worked in a nursery by day and spent the rest of her time looking after her mother who, as her illness progressed, became increasingly difficult.

'A time came when I could no longer cope with earning enough to keep the home going and looking after her, especially as her illness had affected her mentally,' Joy says. The problem was solved when Joy's mother was able to go and live in a Cheshire Home in Hampshire while Joy and her brother went to stay with relatives in Rugby where Joy found more horticultural work which she loved. During the day she wore Wellingtons which she changed for slippers when she got home, the sad fact being that she could no longer wear shoes.

Before long she had to go into hospital for an operation which seemed successful and, confident of her future, she got married at the age of twenty-one. Then the benefit of the operation wore off and after more tests it was found that she was suffering from the same neurological condition as her mother, with the added complication of a circulatory complaint.

The progress of the illness was almost imperceptible over the following years and Joy did manage to lead a reasonably normal life, giving birth to her daughter when she was twenty-seven and to her son a year later. Marital problems began to throw a shadow over her family life, and when she was thirty Joy was forced to seek a divorce. For the next three years she looked after the two childen alone which became more and more difficult as the disease advanced and forced her to use crutches.

Looking back on that difficult time, Joy says, 'It was terrible when the children were little and I had to send them up to bed alone. I just could not get upstairs to tuck them in and kiss them goodnight.'

Joy's condition worsened dramatically in 1977 and, after being admitted to hospital, she realized she would not be able to look after her children in the future and steeled herself to make arrangements for having them fostered. It was the same heartbreaking decision that Heather Strudwick had faced twenty years earlier. And Joy's spirits were further lowered on the September of the following year when it was found necessary to amputate her leg. In 1980 her other leg had to be removed and, to make matters even worse, her ability to use her arms and hands was failing.

When the doctors decided there was nothing more they could do for her, the problem was what to be done with someone in her condition. It seemed that because of the nature of her illness she did not fit neatly into any particular category and as a result found herself being moved from pillar to post. Despite the fact that she was still a young woman she spent two years in a geriatric hospital and, although her complaint was neurological in nature and she was now paralysed, she ended up in the corner of a ward devoted to cardiac cases.

She remembers that she was miserable for weeks. In looking after the cardiac cases the staff were far too busy to attend to her, and sometimes she would lie for half a day waiting for a drink. Having reached a stage where she could no longer turn the page of a book, she found it impossible to escape her surroundings by reading as she had in the past.

Hope was renewed when she managed to get herself sent to the Mary Marlborough Lodge, a residential unit attached to the Nuffield Orthopaedic Hospital just outside Oxford, and here she was provided with an electric wheelchair which she could control with the small amount of movement in her left hand. Three months later this movement was lost, and once more Joy was confined to bed. She finally found herself in the Hospital of St Cross in Rugby. Here, in 1982, the registrar who was anxious about Joy and the seemingly aimless life she was forced to lead, suggested to her that she should do something with her time — such as writing or drawing.

Although she now had no use in her arms, the idea seized Joy's imagination and with the aid of the occupational therapist she was strapped into a wheelchair for hour-long periods while she endeavoured to come to terms with a piece of paper pinned to hardboard, a box of children's water-colours and a brush that was placed in her mouth.

'I set to work as best I could and the first thing that I did was a Christmas card with a candle and a piece of holly round the bottom,' she recalls. 'Although I say it myself it was good — had it been awful I would never have tried again.'

Christmas was seven weeks away and Joy decided that this year she would paint her own cards. In order to do this she forced herself to spend longer and longer strapped painfully in her wheelchair but she achieved her aim and by the middle of December she had produced twenty-six cards, a few that she particularly liked she decided to keep for herself.

As it turned out this was a fortunate decision. Joy's therapist told her that she ought to contact the Association of Mouth and Foot Painting Artists. Joy only knew of them because her mother used to buy their cards and the thought that they might be interested in her seemed ludicrous.

'I had only been painting for three months,' she explains, 'and I could not do anything large because I was unable to control long-handled brushes, and because of the nature of my disability I do not have the reach for wide pictures.'

Nevertheless the therapist had her way and a reply came from the Association asking for some samples of Joy's work. How thankful she was that she had kept some of her cards which impressed the Association's panel of judges so much that despite the short time she had been painting she was invited to become a student. Two years later she was made a full member.

'Joining the Association was a turning point for me,' Joy says. 'Apart from anything else it meant I could save up to buy my present electric wheelchair, the seat of which was made for me at the Mary Marlborough Lodge in Oxford. It enabled me to sit up for long periods — which gradually became all day — in relative comfort and in an orthopaedically correct position.'

And after being adrift for so long in different hospitals Joy realized her dream of independence by moving into her own home. In Rugby the Social Services found her a disused bungalow which stood in the grounds of what had once been a home for the elderly. Despite its neglected appearance she fell in love with it at first sight, no doubt because its weed-filled garden awakened her horticultural instincts.

Today the bungalow has been transformed into a delightful home which Joy shares with a large number of house plants. When she first moved in there was no furniture or carpets but a grant from the Association helped her to furnish it. In her special electric chair — controlled by mechanism activated by pressure from her chin — Joy is able to travel from room to room and position herself in front of her easel for work sessions in the spare room which is now a studio.

Joy happily lives on her own with nurses coming in the morning to get her up and in the evening to put her to bed, and three mornings a week a helper comes in from the Crossroads scheme to do the housework. Her great delight is the garden she has created from a wilderness. Obviously it is impossible for her to do the physical work herself and she has to employ someone to do it for her, but she has the fun of planning it and going out to buy the plants in her electric wheelchair.

One of the pleasures of having her own home again is that she can entertain her children who visit her regularly and do their bit in the garden when there is weeding or planting to be done. The flowers grown there are often the inspiration for her paintings and she says, 'You have to love the things you paint.'

Since she moved into the bungalow and proved that she is capable of an independent life Joy still has had problems to face. She has to take drugs each day to keep pain at bay, and she has been to hospital for more operations, yet she somehow retains an enthusiasm for life that shines through in her delicate paintings.

ALEX CRAIG

Making the most of a bad joke

Like several other artists mentioned in this book, Alex Craig became paralysed from the neck down as the result of a diving accident. The eldest son of six children with a Scots father and Samoan mother, Alex was born in Auckland in 1957. In 1974 he was about to start his fifth form year at St Paul's College when swimming at Don Bucks Creek in Massey he dived into the water and struck a submerged rock ledge.

'I spent four years at Auckland Hospital and then transferred to the Otara Spinal Unit for another four,' he explains. 'It was during the time I spent at Auckland Hospital that I met a person called Bruce Hopkins who happened to be a member of the Mouth and Foot Painting Artists Association and we developed a friendship that we maintained until he died. He tried to introduce me to mouth painting but at that stage I wasn't interested. Prior to my accident art was purely a hobby and I wanted to keep it that way.'

However Bruce Hopkins continued in his attempts to persuade the young man to take up painting as an antidote to the long listless hours which can be so tedious for those who are sentenced to life in a wheelchair. Finally he was successful though Alex found it very difficult to control the brush at first.

'I found there are many brush strokes that can be done only by hand and not by mouth,' he says. 'My neck became very sore with the movements I had to make but with practice I got used to it and I felt more comfortable as my neck muscles developed.'

After countless hours of labour at his easel Alex finally produced twelve pictures which he felt were of a high enough standard to submit to the Association. He now says that the problem with his painting then was that he was suffering a long period of depression and his work tended to reflect his mood. If this was so his pictures did not depress the Association's panel of professional artists and in 1980 Alex was awarded a scholarship.

During the last ten years I have been in numerous exhibitions around the country and in publications throughout New Zealand and Australia,' Alex says. 'I have been involved with many well known New Zealand artists by way of workshops but the biggest influence on my style was Bruce Hopkins. After his death Doreen Jones (who is mentioned elsewhere in this book) took it a stage further with her encouragement and expertise.'

Today Alex bases his paintings on life and scenery around him like most able-bodied artists though when necessary he will research ideas in libraries. What is remarkable is the life of independence that he has forged for himself. If he wants to go out and paint some of New Zealand's splendid scenery he can drive to it in his own specially adapted car though he does need assistance to get in and out of the vehicle.

'When I go anywhere I either have someone with me or arrange someone to meet me at my destination,' he explains. 'There have been times when I have gone somewhere and through lack of organisation on my part I have had to call upon a member of the public to assist me, and I must admit that in New Zealand people appear only too willing to help when needed.'

Having been institutionalized for eight years of his life, Alex now lives on his own with a nurse coming each morning to help him get up and organise his daily routine, and returning in the evening to help him to bed. Being on his own he tends to eat out a lot which makes him very appreciative of home-cooked meals.

According to Alex, the secret of living in the community if one is disabled is to spread the workload in regards to helpers.

'By depending on one or a few persons, they tend to be overtaxed,' Alex declares. 'You must be aware of what resources are available to you and tap into them. It is also important to be seen helping oneself. If a member of the public is interested enough to enquire about my disability, I take the time to explain and make a good impression, so when they meet the next disabled person it helps them to be more at ease.

'I go to the Otara Spinal Unit and do counselling for the new recruits and keep up to date with any new information from overseas. I feel this is a two-way thing where I am putting back into the system what I got out.'

Alex admits that he finds work as an artist can be a lonely 'hermit style' occupation. Being of Polynesian descent — and Polynesians are noted for their social orientation — he has to balance his solitary working life with activities which keep him in touch with other people which includes coaching third division men's basketball, going to the races, playing most board games, attending Rugby matches and enjoying 'walks' in his electric wheelchair in the local park. He also finds time to be a member of the local paraplegic association and serve on the committee of his local basketball association.

'In regards to my disability I don't accept it, I just make the most of a bad joke,' Alex says. 'I let the high times get me through the low times. A good sense of humour is a must. I feel that to communicate with someone who is healthy in mind and body and for them to associate with someone with a disability, you must first get past the myth that someone physically disabled must therefore be mentally disabled.'

PAUL DRIVER

A full spread of canvas

Paul Driver is an artist who draws his inspiration from the things he loved before he became disabled — the sea and the vessels that sail upon it. Speaking of his life as a young man he says, 'I learned to sail a dinghy on the River Blackwater and spent many holiday on the Norfolk Broads. Sailing was to me the purest pleasure I knew, whether I was trying in a dinghy to coax steerage way from an almost non-existent breeze or hanging on the shuddering tiller of a thirty-footer with the sails full and the wash rushing past the hull. I often thought of my boyhood when, passionately fond of the sea even then, I longed to sail in a windjammer.'

In 1944, at the age of eighteen, Paul had volunteered to join the navy, but to his horror he found that instead of becoming a sailor the authorities, in the form of the Ministry of Labour, decided that he must become a Bevin Boy.

Bevin Boys — they got their nickname from the then Minister of Labour Ernest Bevin — were conscripted to work in mines to maintain Britain's coal production. Originally men were given the choice of going into the services or the coalfields but as most preferred the idea of a rifle to a pick a ballot system was introduced so that a fifth of recruits was drafted to the coalfields.

A disappointed Paul was given a month's training at Creswell Colliery and then sent to the mining village of Eastwood on the Derbyshire border where he worked underground driving pit ponies.

He remained a Bevin Boy for three years during which he used his free time to explore by bicycle the countryside around Nottingham and the Peak District. And after his term as a miner ended the love of the outdoors persisted.

Looking back on his twenties as the good years, Paul says, 'At the beginning I had little money but the things I liked doing — cycling, walking, staying at youth hostels — were not expensive. Alone, or with my younger brother, I covered a large part of England on my bicycle. With friends from my mining days — and some of the friendships I formed then have lasted until today — I visited France and Scotland, and there were long walking tours in Wales, Cornwall and the Lake District.'

And, of course, sailing.

After leaving the pits Paul worked as a clerk in a City office — a job 'boring beyond belief' — and then, having started training as a quantity surveyor before he became a Bevin Boy, he returned to that profession with the London County Council Housing Department. Later he moved to a private firm that had just opened up a new office in Leeds which gave him access to the Yorkshire Moors and the Pennines.

In 1955 a poliomyelitis epidemic spread through Britain. When Paul first felt 'under the weather' he dismissed the symptoms as being those of 'flu, but when he collapsed his landlady called a doctor and within an hour the young man was in the Seacroft Hospital. By now he was to fight for breath and he guessed that he had contracted polio when he was told that he would have to be put in an iron lung. For the next year he remained a prisoner of the machine which kept him alive through its constantly changing air pressure inflating and deflating his lungs.

To pass the time he read a great deal. His head protruded from an airtight collar and books were placed open on a glass shelf fitted above his face. But what absorbed him more than books was having an Ordnance Survey map on the shelf so that he followed the lines of well remembered paths and in imagination once more saw the landscapes he loved.

Paul's progress was better than expected and he worked at using his throat muscles to breathe until it was possible for him to be independent of the lung for periods of eight hours.

He explains, 'I normally breathe with the remaining muscles in the front and side of my neck — the muscles you would use if you were taking extra deep breath. Glossopharengeal breathing ("frog breathing" which is used by Heather Strudwick) is a separate process. It consists of trapping small amounts of air with the soft palate, forcing it down into the lungs and holding it there by closing the larnyx, then repeating the process several times so that the chest is pumped up rather like a bicycle tyre. I do not depend on frog breathing but use it when I need a bit more breath or when I need an extra deep breath such as when I cough.'

Next Paul was transferred to Pinderfields Orthopaedic Hospital where he was given special exercies and began to use a rubber-tipped rod attached to a head harness to turn the pages of his books. Eighteen months after he was taken ill he was able to return to sleeping in an ordinary bed in which he wore a portable respirator while during the day he was able to sit up in a wheelchair. He was moved to the Western Hospital in Fulham, London, so that he could be near his parents, and when his brother got married in the summer of 1957 he was able to attend the wedding.

Although almost completely paralysed at first, physiotherapists managed to coax some movement back to his legs and feet. Earlier on Paul had cherished an ambition to be an author, and now this revived when he began to write with a ballpoint pen which, fixed in a bobbin, he was able to hold between his first and second toe. This method was not successful and he changed to using a typewriter whose keys he pressed with a piece of dowelling taped to his big toe.

The next breakthrough was an apparatus which enabled him to feed himself.

'By a strange coincidence it was invented in New Zealand for a man who not only had the same problem as me but the same surname — Driver,' Paul says. 'Jim Driver, who I later learned was a member of the Association of Mouth and Foot Painting Artists, had a "Distaff". It consisted of a thin metal arm mounted on a metal tube which the user could operate by means of a foot pedal. I cannot tell you what a great delight it was to be able to sit at a dining table and eat under my own steam after having been fed by nurses for so long.'

Although Paul had found it too difficult to write with a ballpoint between his toes, he discovered he could use a brush effectively which enabled him to take up painting as a hobby. His early efforts were understandably crude but he was eager to improve and progressed so well that a hospital chaplain took several of his pictures along to an exhibition at a local library. On hearing of the way that these paintings had been produced, a reporter wrote an article on them for his newspaper. This item finally reached the Association of Mouth and Foot Painting Artists and Paul was asked to submit specimens of his artwork.

Because he felt his painting was too amateurish Paul declined the invitation.

In 1960 he went for a year to the Mary Marlborough Lodge, the new Nuffield Orthopaedic Centre in Oxford, which had been established to assist the disabled to make the most of whatever movement they retained, and here Paul learned to steer an electric wheelchair fitted with foot controls. When this period was over he went to live at the Athol House Cheshire Home in Upper Norwood which was close to his parents' home. As time went on he came to the conclusion that the profession of authorship was not for him despite having worked so hard at it but, as though to compensate for this, he found that his painting had progressed until it was something more serious than a hobby. He remembered the interest the Association of Mouth and Foot Painting Artists had shown in him some years earlier and now he had enough confidence in his work to send in some samples for evaluation by the Association's artistic panel.

In 1966 he became a student which meant he could now afford private tuition, studying composition and techniques which involved changing from water-colours to oils. In order to compare his work with that of able-bodied students he became a member of an evening portrait class. Five years later his work earned him full membership and from then on he was financially independent and able to afford his own fees at Athol House.

In 1975 Paul married a girl from Switzerland and two years later the first of their two sons were born, the second arriving in 1979. The couple moved into a flat in a block specially built by the Greater London Council to be accessible for wheelchairs. A room in the flat overlooks a grassy garden with pleasant trees, and this is Paul's studio where he works practically every day. The walls are decorated with his paintings and there are piles of reference books so that he can check that the details of the old time ships he loves to paint are correct.

Paul works in a wheelchair from which the footrests have been removed. His easel is set at a tilted angle on a chair and an extra large palette is placed on the floor below. When it comes to mixing paint on it he does not need to have someone come and unscrew the caps from his paint tubes, he merely keeps uncapped tubes upside down in jars of water which prevents the oil paint from drying. From childhood Paul has been fascinated by ships — as a boy his greatest desire was to sail on a windjammer — and now that fascination is captured on his evocative marine canvases.

JIM DUNCAN

Forever striving for independence

New Zealand in the early 'thirties was in the grip of the Great Depression and hunger was not unknown despite the fact that production of food was the main occupation of the country. But what was feared more than the spectre of unemployment was the periodic epidemics of poliomyelitis which was then known by the chilling name of Infantile Paralysis. In those pre-Salk days there was no protection or cure, and as soon as cases were reported schools across the country would be closed in order to cut down the risk of the infection spreading.

There was a belief among mothers of young children that a small block of camphor worn in a little bag on a tape round the neck would offer protection. Today this may be looked back upon as a curious piece of folklore but then, when panic headlines in the newspapers reported increasing cases, anything seemed worth trying. Even now the chance smell of camphor transports the memory of the author back to childhood days when one dared not venture out without one's camphor bag. The consequential licking of the block became a habit which gave no pleasure other than satisfaction of having been forbidden to do it.

At this time Jim Duncan was born in the town of Napier which was still recovering from the severe earthquake of 1931. He grew up in the Hawke's Bay countryside and after completing high school he went out into the world to find a career that suited him. Like many young New Zealanders of his day he was ready to try anything and in the early 'fifties jobs were not hard to come by. He was a cub reporter on a newspaper in Wellington until the lure of the countryside made him give up the city life for farming. This led to truck driving, contract firewood cutting and then taking a senior apprenticeship in carpentry.

Jim found this work much to his liking but there was something in his nature which made him eager to meet a challenge and so, when he was qualified in carpentry, he then began to work in engineering. He married happily and was to become a father of four daughters who today he still likes to describe as beautiful.

In 1961 his wife was three months pregnant with the child destined to be their only son who would be named James after his father. Coming home from work Jim complained of a headache and soon this developed into symptoms the like of which he had never experienced before. It did not take the local doctor long to guess the cause and Jim was rushed to a hospital in Auckland where poliomyelitis was diagnosed.

The action of the polio virus causes inflammation of the anterior horn cells of the spinal cord which govern muscle action and thus paralysis is produced in the patient, usually affecting the limbs and in severe cases the whole body. In Jim's case he was paralysed from the waist up and added to this was the terrifying fact that he found he was unable to breathe.

'In hospital I was put on a respirator with a tracheotomy tube in my windpipe to enable me to breathe,' he says. 'I was unable to talk and my arms and hands had hardly a flicker of movement. But with paper on a board at the end of my bed I found that I was able to communicate.'

This was done by means of a pencil held in his toes and when the worst onslaught of the illness was over he was able to sit by his bed, still attached to the respirator by a tube to his throat, and teach himself to type with his feet.

As he became more skilful with this method Jim began to experiment on drawing with coloured pencils in order to relieve the tedium of hospital life. His occupational therapist was impressed with his unexpected talent and contact was made with the Association of Mouth and Foot Painting Artists which had just been established in New Zealand. Examples of his work were sent to the headquarters of the Association in Vaduz, Liechtenstein, but to Jim's disappointment they were returned with a letter saying they were not suitable as the Association only used paintings for its cards and calendars.

'I decided to begin painting properly,' says Jim. 'On my first attempt nurses set up paints, brushes, water and paper for me but I only did two strokes before I tipped the lot over the bed. I was disgusted with myself and I thought I would never be a painter.

'After eight months working on all available muscles not affected by polio, I managed to breathe on my own. My tracheotomy was closed and I left hospital. Twelve months went by and I decided to have another try at painting. I was driven by the thought that if I could reach a high enough standard and become a member of the Association I would be able to support my family instead of being dependent on Government assistance.'

For a while Jim employed a tutor but this did not work well as he found he was too slow for his teacher and after that he taught himself. Finally he had six water-colours which satisfied him enough to submit to the Association with the result that he was enrolled as a student and given a monthly grant to buy art materials.

'Five years and hundreds of gradually improving water-colours later, plus many exhibitions up and down the country, the Association granted me full membership,' he says. 'With the money from the sales of my paintings overseas and my salary I managed to save up to buy our own home.'

It was at this time that Jim switched from watercolours to oil paints which he found more satisfactory. He also moved from New Zealand to Australia, settling in 1980 on the Gold Coast of Queensland to enjoy the climate and the sea, and to continue his art career. He saw his family grow up with the satisfaction of having been able to provide despite his paralysis rather than be a liability. Then, in 1986, his breathing capability suddenly deteriorated and by the time he entered hospital he was unconscious.

'Another tracheotomy operation was performed,' Jim says. 'Another tube was inserted in my windpipe which allows me to keep my lungs clear and enables me to hook up to a respirator to sleep at night. My wife, who is still a pillar of strength after nursing me all these years, wanted me home. Southport Hospital discharged me with a respirator and Monica has the job of nursing me back to health again. I am extremely lucky as of the family three are married and all are very close and loving.

'Depite my disability I have accomplished a number of activities that once I would have thought impossible, the one I am most proud of is being able to drive my car with a foot control that I designed myself. I have held my licence for over twenty years and have driven hundreds of thousands of miles.

'I am forever striving for independence.'

ALEXANDER CRAIG
Gold Glory
Oil   40 x 30 cm

ALEXANDER CRAIG
Finch
Oil   51 x 40 cm

ALEXANDER CRAIG
Blue Flowers
Oil   41 x 30 cm

82

PAUL DRIVER
Sailing Boats
Oil   61 x 51 cm

83

PAUL DRIVER *Winter in Switzerland* Oil 41 x 50 cm

PAUL DRIVER *Regatta* Oil

PAUL DRIVER   *Tower Bridge*   Oil   34 x 44 cm

PAUL DRIVER   *Winter Sunrise*   Oil   41 x 50 cm

JAMES CLAUDE DUNCAN   *Mountain Landscape*   Oil   35 x 35 cm

JAMES CLAUDE DUNCAN
Brook Landscape
Oil   50 x 40 cm

JAMES CLAUDE DUNCAN
Coastal Landscape
Oil   41 x 50 cm

JAMES CLAUDE DUNCAN   *Mountain Lake Scene*   Oil   40 x 50 cm

JAMES CLAUDE DUNCAN   *Serenity Scene*   Oil

CHARLES FOWLER   *The Beach*   Watercolour   14 x 19 cm

Overleaf: CHARLES FOWLER   *Landscape*   Watercolour

CHARLES FOWLER   *Small Lake*   Watercolour   37 x 56 cm

CHARLES FOWLER   *Woodland Stream*   Watercolour   37 x 55 cm

CHARLES FOWLER   *Cliff Scene*   Watercolour   39 x 57 cm

CHARLES FOWLER   *Sea Landscape*   Watercolour

Overleaf: MARGARET GREIG   *Frozen Winter Landscape*   Oil   40 x 61 cm

CHARLES FOWLER   *Cool Day, Autumn (Ireland)*   Oil   46 x 71 cm

MARGARET GREIG
Zinnias
Oil   51 x 38 cm

MARGARET GREIG
Meditation
Oil   29 x 29 cm

CHARLES FOWLER

'The sheer sense of not worrying.'

'And have you seen Charles lately?' It was the question most often put to the author of this book when travelling about England to interview members of the Mouth and Foot Painting Artists. One thing he found was the lively interest they take in each other, having met at the Association's exhibitions, usually held twice a year, and conferences.

The member who is best known to them is the elegant and quietly spoken Charles Fowler, not only because of the promotional work he does for the Association and the arranging of exhibitions but because of the genuine interest he takes in his fellow members.

It is not unusual for a student's telephone to ring and there is Charles on the line to ask how they are getting on, give words of encouragement and, if necessary, advice. To the younger students he is a father figure, both kindly and critical in a positive way.

It is a role he is well fitted for because until he joined the Association of Mouth and Foot Painting Artists in 1975 he made his living as a lecturer at the Farnham School of Art despite the fact that he had lost both arms at the age of eighteen when he slipped from the door of a railway carriage at Wimbledon Station.

Prior to this he had been a clerk in the linseed oil trade, though because of his interest in drawing at school he had considered applying for a place in an art school. However, practical considerations prevailed — until after his accident.

It was after he returned to his parents' home following his spell in hospital that the urge to paint returned to him, and he began to experiment holding a brush in his mouth. Today he says that he found it less difficult than one might think because he was very young and therefore it was easier for him to adapt.

'And I was helped by the sheer sense of not worrying,' he says. 'I had the quality of acceptance as most disabled people do.'

Once Charles had accustomed himself to the new technique he happened to paint a study of a May tree in blossom. It appealed so much to those who saw it that he received many offers of cash for it.

The idea of being able to earn money through his mouth-held brush was an exhilarating one and Charles went into a mass-production painting business, working on seven identical May tree pictures at a time. Inspired by the success of his May tree, he decided to do what he had always wanted to do and take up art. The first step was to take lessons from a professional. This entailed a railway journey but Charles refused to be daunted by his horrific memory of Wimbledon Station and, rather than be dependent on fellow passengers, he worked out a way of opening carriage doors with his foot.

Later he attended an art school for four years and won an Exhibition Scholarship to the Royal College of Art. The painting profession is one of the most difficult in which to make a living and though Charles' pictures were hung in many illustrious galleries, including the Royal Academy, he felt the need to earn a regular income and so began lecturing in still life at the Farnham School of Art. From here he took the post of an evening lecturer at the Richmond Institute, an ideal situation for Charles as it gave him the daytime to work at his own painting. Ultimately he became Head of the Richmond Institute's Art Department and remained in this position for fifteen years until he retired from teaching in 1975.

Retirement for Charles did not mean hanging up his palette. Having heard of the Mouth and Foot Painting Artists, he visited the Association's office in London and, impressed by the work he saw there, submitted some pictures for consideration. The result was that he was immediately granted full membership.

During the 1988 MFPA Delegates' Conference held in London he was elected to the Board by unanimous vote and now travels to Liechtenstein twice yearly to attend Board meetings. A short while before this he was asked, along with fellow artist Paul Driver and H.H. Marcus, to become a trustee for the Association's Trust Fund for the Training of Handicapped Children in the Arts, which in effect means he is the principal trustee deciding on and making awards to individual children or special schools.

Despite his busy schedule Charles continues as enthusiastically as ever with his life-long love of art. One has only to look at the bright, light-filled paintings of Charles Fowler to appreciate his love of landscape. He travels extensively to places where as yet nature has not been sullied by the so-called needs of the 20th century, such as Sark in the Channel Islands.

'I am an Atlantic rather than a Mediterranean person,' he says. 'I love feeling the power of the wind and watching the movement of the sea.'

Charles makes pencil sketches of the scenes he wishes to capture and if there are no spectators there is nothing more he likes than painting on the spot.

'It's strange that, after all this time, I get a little unsure when I know there are people about watching me. I know it's silly but I'm not like Erich Stegmann who couldn't care less who was watching him. What a wonderful man he was. I count myself lucky to have met him on several occasions.'

MARGARET GREIG

There is also happiness

The nurse looked down at the paralysed girl resting on her stomach after an exhausting physiotherapy session and said, 'If you miss your folks, why don't you try writing home to them.'

To an outsider such a remark to a quadriplegic patient would have sounded callous to say the least but the nurse knew what she was doing. Without waiting for a reply, she put the end of a ballpoint pen into the patient's mouth and positioned a writing pad in front of her face.

Recounting the experience to the author, Margaret Greig said, 'The result was lines of squiggles across the paper. They would have probably put most people off but they fascinated me. It was the first thing I had been able to do for myself since I had been out of an iron lung, and it encouraged me enough to try harder each day until my "writing" became legible enough for me to really write home. At that time I did not know about artists who painted by mouth or foot, but this form of writing led to my attempts at drawing which was something I had enjoyed at school.'

Margaret's first sketches were of horses drawn from memory of the horses she had loved on the family farm in Moruya on the southern coast of New South Wales. Lying in Sydney's Prince Henry Hospital, faraway Moruya now seemed like a golden dream to the girl whose life had been idyllic there.

One of a large and happy family of four girls and three boys Margaret was born in 1937 on her parents' dairy farm on the unspoilt pastureland for which the area is famous.

'There was never an abundance of money in the family,' she recalls, 'but we were all happy and overflowing with health and high spirits.' And a natural way of life that most would envy in these over mechanized, pollution-threatened times. There were no tractors on the Greig farm, their work was done by great woolly-footed shire horses who had no objection to providing rides for their master's lively children.

Horses were Margaret's abiding love. There was nothing she liked better than to take the family pony and wander at will over the surrounding countryside, and on the same pony she won prizes for riding at the local agricultural show.

Ever since she could remember it was Margaret's ambition to become a nurse when she was old enough but it was an ambition that was never to be fulfilled. One day in 1950 Margaret complained of a terrible headache. It was a time when poliomyelitis was having one of its periodic epidemics in Australia and, in the days before the introduction of Salk vaccine, parents across the country were on the alert for tell-tale symptoms. A doctor was urgently called to the Greig farm and as soon as he saw the thirteen-year-old girl he arranged for an ambulance to rush her to hospital.

Already she was finding it difficult to breathe and as soon as she was admitted to hospital she was placed in an iron lung. There could be no doubt that she had contracted polio.

Looking back on the moment when the airtight collar of the breathing apparatus was sealed round her neck Margaret says, 'I was so sick I was past caring. In fact, it was a relief to be in it. Then, as I began to recover, though still without movement, it didn't occur to me that I wouldn't be going home and doing the things I had always done. By the time it did I had already accepted my disability.'

Instead of going home, Margaret was sent for specialist treatment to the Prince Henry Hospital over two hundred miles away in Sydney, and more than three years were to pass before she saw Moruya again.

After some time in the Sydney hospital she was cheered by the fact that she had recovered sufficiently to begin a course of physiotherapy and after fifteen months she achieved some limited use of her arms but not of her hands or legs and it was obvious that she would be confined to a wheelchair for the rest of her life. It was at this point that she began writing with a ballpoint pen held in her mouth and this enabled her to take a correspondence course while still in hospital.

Impressed by her brave attempts to draw, the nursing staff gave her a set of water-colours but she found trying to control the brush was a frustrating business when unwanted dribbles of colour marred her attempts.

When her schooling was completed by her correspondence lessons a friend suggested she took another postal course to keep herself occupied. Ticket writing was chosen as this would fit in with her increasing skill with a mouth-held pen. Margaret enrolled but found part of the work difficult because her neck movement was very limited and this restricted the range of her pen. Nevertheless she succeeded in completing the course and her patient determination was repaid by the fact that the ticket-writing exercises taught her how to use both brush and pen with greater control — which proved invaluable later.

At last Margaret was allowed to return to Moruya where she would be looked after by her parents. It is hard to describe the emotion she felt when she gazed out over the farm where once she had done her share of chores, looked after the Fresian calves with her brothers and sisters, and galloped so free on her pony. Nearly four years had passed since then and life had changed completely *but she was home again*!

Speaking of that time she says, 'I busied myself with many interests but there was nothing available that would enable me to take up some sort of employment or earn a living for myself.'

As the years passed Mrs Greig's health began to decline and Margaret had to face up to one of the most difficult decisions that can confront disabled people. Knowing that it would be increasingly hard for her mother to care for her she chose to leave the farm where she had been so happy and, with many private misgivings, she arranged to enter a home for the disabled in Penrith near Sydney.

Many of these misgivings proved to be unfounded. Margaret soon found herself enjoying the camaraderie that existed among those who shared the common experience of disablement. It also meant that she was able to work for the first time as the home had a sheltered workshop where inmates could perform tasks according to whatever physical ability they retained. From here Margaret graduated to the administrator's office where she typed on an electric machine by pressing the keys with the tip of a mouthstick. She says that she found it thrilling to be employed at last, but an even bigger challenge came when she was asked to become a Sunday School teacher.

Margaret had always been a Christian and had found comfort in her faith during her darkest hours — on the wall of her studio today is a Bible text from the Philippians

'For I have learned in whatever state I am, therewith to be content.' While the idea of teaching appealed to her, the practicality of it was worrying. How would the children react to being taught by someone in a wheelchair without the use of her arms and legs?

In reality her sunny nature soon made her charges forget her disability, and through her new activity she joined the Christian Fellowship. Here she made friends with a woman named Mel Fleming who one day brought her a set of oil paints, explaining that they had belonged to her husband who had tried to take up painting as a hobby only to find that it did not live up to his expectations.

Mel knew that Margaret had never been happy with water-colours and she thought that oils might be more suitable. Her idea was confirmed the moment Margaret's mouth-held brush spread the vivid and pliable paint over her canvas. At that moment she felt a whole new prospect was opening up. With her enthusiasm for painting rekindled she devoted herself to mastering the exciting new medium. Word of her endeavours reached the Association of Mouth and Foot Painting Artists and she was invited to send in samples of her work.

After these had been evaluated Margaret was offered a studentship by the Association — 'the real turning point in my life,' she says today. She had tremendous satisfaction in writing to the Social Security Department to inform them that she no longer needed financial assistance now that she had her student's grant.

Her aim was to become a fully-fledged member and to this end she worked at her painting so enthusiastically that her room in the home became stacked with canvases. There was no doubt about it, like any other artist she needed a studio and in 1972 her friend Mel came to her aid. She and her husband invited Margaret to share their home in Londonderry, New South Wales, where a studio was built for her on an adjoining plot of land.

Following her hard work Margaret did become a full member and arrangements were made for an exhibition of her work with that of fellow Association artist Bruce Peardon, to be mounted in Newcastle, New South Wales, where they would demonstrate the mouth-painting technique. To be suddenly the focus of attention filled her with apprehension but when Bruce calmly started painting with a crowd round him she plucked up courage and followed his example and as once more she was filled with the old magic of oil paint and canvas she forgot the spectators and became absorbed in her picture.

Ten years after she had gone to live with the Flemings, Margaret, thanks to her earnings as an artist, built a house on the plot next door to her friends. She moved in with a companion, Marie Kelly, who was a teacher of handicapped children, plus a number of pets which included two goats, two donkeys, three dogs and Prince a miniature horse just over thirty-one inches high. With her animals for company Margaret not only works in her studio but also entertains visitors who come to see — and buy — her paintings which are on permanent display. Each August she holds a special exhibition to raise funds for St George's Association for the Disabled which provides visits and holiday accommodation for the handicapped.

Once it seemed that to have her own home was an impossible dream but it is not the only one that has come true — Margaret has been able to travel both in Australia and round the world.

'After I had contracted polio the last thing I thought I would ever be able to do would be to go camping,' she said referring both to her trips at home and in Europe with friends. 'But I found travel in a camper is more convenient than staying in hotels. Few are suited to accommodating disabled people with wheelchairs and this is especially difficult when you are unable to get a room on the ground floor, but you can adapt a camper to your needs.'

In 1985 Margaret flew to England before attending a Mouth and Foot Painting Artists' conference in Madrid, and the highlight of her holiday was a visit to the Kilverstone Wildlife Park in Norfolk which is a centre for miniature horses. Horses still mean a great deal to her and are the subjects of many of her paintings, as well as vivid scenes of Australian landscape with its unique timeless quality — both subjects which go back to her carefree girlhood. Yet, though a horse can now only be a pet, and the countryside viewed only from a wheelchair, Margaret is adamant that if disablement was to be her fate so also is happiness.

KRIS KIRK

Some magic in the world

Despite the fact that Kris Kirk has to spend his waking life in a wheelchair there is an aura of restless energy about him. The breadth of his shoulders still suggest the athlete and he paints with the same determination that as a youth he devoted to sport — once he almost made it into the England Junior Rugby Team.

In 1973 he enjoyed great success on the games field; at school he was captain of the cricket, baseball and Rugby teams, and it was in the latter game that he represented London, Middlesex and South East England. All this ended abruptly when, during a family outing at Brighton, fifteen-year-old Kris dived off a groyne and his head struck the sandy bottom.

'When I came up to the surface I opened my eyes and found that I could not move,' he says. 'My body refused to obey me and I just floated.'

His cousin realized there was something wrong and brought him ashore where he lay on the beach unable to move. An ambulance was called and Kris was taken to Brighton Hospital where his family was told that his neck was broken. After two days in traction he was taken to Stoke Mandeville Hospital for specialized treatment which was to last for a year. Every effort was made by physiotherapists to bring back the use of his muscles but to no avail. When the specialists had to admit that he would never have control over his hands again, various gadgets were tried by which it was hoped he would be able to write by using the slight movement that was left in his arm.

Although ingenious, these devices were too complicated for Kris and he knew that if he used them he would always need someone to fit them to him. In the end it was decided to see if he could learn to write by the far less complicated method of holding a pencil in his mouth. In the occupational therapy department he began to practise the technique.

'They thought it would be useful if I could write letters,' Kris explains. 'At that time, even though I had taken an O-level in art, it did not occur to me that there was any future for me as an artist. But once when I was not busy practising the alphabet I did try a drawing. It was of a lion, but as to how good it was I can only say that when my doctor came on his rounds and saw it he quoted, "Tyger, Tyger burning bright. . . " '

After Stoke Mandeville Kris returned to his family in London, and found it to be very supportive. Although he is English born, his parents came from Cyprus and they retained the strong Greek Cypriot sense of family. In order that he should continue his studies, lessons were brought to his home by teachers. One of these was an art teacher and when he saw the progress the disabled youth was making in the subject with a mouth-held pencil he arranged for him to go to college once a week. The result was that Kris got an A-level in art, and after this Rehab, a Government-backed organization, arranged for an art teacher to visit him regularly.

Kris was grateful for this help but now admits that the work he was expected to do was not very exciting.

'I was doing art but sometimes it would take me weeks to draw a potato on a plate,' he says.

Kris had several Rehab teachers, and it was the final one named Fred Bloomfield who had a tremendous effect upon him.

'He's an incredible artist,' Kris says. 'He likes to paint surreal subjects best, and sometimes he'll work on a canvas for a year until it's perfect. He was — and still is — a real friend. He gave me loads of technical advice, and even suggested that someday I might make a living out of painting.'

In 1978 Kris remembered that a physiotherapist had once told him about the Mouth and Foot Painting Artists and now he decided to approach the Association. In response to his letter Kris was visited by Charles Fowler who looked carefully through his paintings, selecting four to take away for the Association to assess.

'Then at Christmas I received word from the Association and it was the best Christmas present I ever had,' says Kris. 'They were willing to take me on as a student which meant that I would be helped financially, art materials would be provided and if necessary a teacher would be employed to help me improve my standard. And for me the great thing was that I would be able to work at home.'

At that time much of Kris's work was surrealistic, reflecting the influence of his teacher Fred Bloomfield, and now that he had been accepted as a student he knew he would have to tackle other forms of painting.

'After all, you can't have surreal calendar and Christmas card illustrations,' he says.

The thing that mattered most in his life was to improve his painting so that he would be accepted as a member of the Association. To this end he started work each morning at ten o'clock with his palette and paints laid out in front of his easel and a brush held firmly in his teeth, and, with only a break of half an hour, he would paint on until seven at night when he was usually so fatigued he could not do any more. Such a regime made him one of the most prolific mouth painters and every three months he submitted on average sixteen of his best paintings. His tremendously hard work paid off in 1982 when he achieved his ambition of full membership.

'That was the best thing that has happened to me since my accident,' he says. 'The Association is so caring. I often suffer with kidney infection as a result of being immobilized and while I am being treated for it I find it impossible to paint, yet I am not made to feel that I am letting them down.'

Becoming a member gave Kris financial security and enabled him to afford to make a pilgrimage to the island he had heard so much about since childhood — Cyprus, the home of his forebears whose name was Kyriacou. He did not fly there as he decided that travelling overland with his family across Europe in his own transport would give him freedom to travel about the island (or at least the Greek section) when they arrived.

Kris recalls, 'The bad part of the journey was before we actually set off — there was so much to think of. My special mattresses had to be taken with us as well as a lot of medical equipment. But once we were on our way I felt fine, and rather than have the problems which might arise with me staying at strange hotels, we camped out which added to the fun. We spent nights in Belgium, Germany, Yugoslavia and Greece. Then we had a two-day voyage to Cyprus where we stayed for six weeks. It was the first time I had ever visited the place where my Mum and Dad came from and I met my relatives for the first time. It was great — and upsetting, and the experience of a lifetime.'

In talking to the author, Kris described how he was taken to a monastery where he found a number of monks in heavy black robes sitting outside and patiently painting icons. Suffering from the heat himself, he wondered how these religious artists managed to stay cool enough to paint in their stifling clothing but he did not stay long enough to find the answer.

The monks had an apiary nearby and the number of bees hovering around the wheelchair 'frightened the living daylights' out of Kris. He tells it as an amusing anecdote but it does underline the plight of the paralysed. For the able-bodied the wave of a hand is usually good enough protection against flies, mosquitoes and wasps, but a person like Kris has no personal defence against the insect world and this can be a problem not only to him but all disabled artists who like to paint out of doors.

Cyprus made such an impact on Kris that he has now made his home there though he makes frequent visits to England. For this he is grateful to the Mouth and Foot Painting Artists.

'If you are disabled like me you have to make money to get what you need, and the Association enables you to do this,' he explains. 'If I had not been working for them I would never have been able to go to Cyprus in the first place. It offers more than a job — it's like a social service. Ordinary people do not worry how they are going out for a walk or maybe visit a beach, but if you are paralysed and you haven't got a van, and if you haven't got a wheelchair fitted so that you can control it yourself, you have to stay at home all the time.'

Like many other disabled people Kris gets a lot of comfort and companionship from his pet — in his case a Doberman pinscher named Czar who has been with him since he was a pup. Before his accident he had Lad, a Collie who he still misses.

'When Lad died at the age of fourteen I had never felt so devastated,' Kris says. 'People might think it's silly to have been so upset over an animal but he was special. Lad was closer to me than Czar can be because he could remember how I used to romp with him before my accident, which is something that I can never do with Czar. When I was in Stoke Mandeville Lad was brought to see me in the grounds of the hospital. I hadn't seen him for a long time but he ran over to me and there was great joy between us.

'He had got lost while I was away, and then he was found at the Battersea Dogs' Home. He had caught a disease that nearly killed him but when the vet wanted to put him down my Mum wouldn't let him because she knew what Lad meant to me and she managed to nurse him through. When he was better he was brought to see me and I vividly remember how cracked the skin of his nose was — funny the little things that come back to you.'

Today Kris continues to work as hard as ever though at times he has to leave off to go to hospital — on average he spends three months a year there with medical problems — and he usually completes a painting once a fortnight. He works in oils with short-handled brushes which give him more control of the paint though this does strain his eyesight through working with his face close to the canvas. 'I put my paintings straight on to the canvas after drawing the outlines in paint — not pencil — and in my mind I know exactly what I want to do,' he explains. 'I like very controlled, tight paintings. Every speck of paint I put down I put there deliberately — not because the brush happened to hit there.'

Speaking of the effect disability has had on his life Kris says that if his accident had not happened he would probably have got married — and then adds, 'But a lot of people who are married regret it, so it's hard to say . . .

'What I do regret is not being able to play sport, especially as a lot of my friends who I went to school with still take part in it. For me Rugby was not just a game, it was a way of life at the Christopher Wren School I went to. The head boy was always a Rugby player and this was nearly always the case with prefects. You got privileges if you were good at Rugby and you got on better with the teachers. Although it was a London comprehensive it was Rugby mad and I loved it.

'I find it's best not to dwell on the past, if you thought about it too much you'd go crazy. I just concentrate on the things that I am good at today and keep them to the forefront. I can't play Rugby any more but I play a lot of chess — sometimes by telephone with Charles Fowler. And I can give my computer a good game.

'I like to think there is some magic in the world. I'd like to think that unicorns once existed . . . And it's the same with religion, I prefer to believe. No one can say definitely whether there is a God or life after death, but those who do believe do have the consolation and uplift of their faith through life and if they are wrong and there is nothing it does not matter because they will never know . . .

'But I must admit that there have been times when I thought God has been unfair but then how can one expect life to be perfect? I think I am unlucky compared with many people and very lucky compared with a lot of others. People often say it but it is true, there is always someone worse off than you. And I think of this when I see famine pictures from Ethiopia, and when I've encountered dossers down the road and have seen drug addicts whose minds are completely gone, I wonder what the hell I'm complaining about.'

ERICH KRELL

An unlimited world

Erich Krell has lived a vivid life and his recounting of it is equally vivid. For example, this is how he has described his childhood in Hitler's Berlin, 'It was the dawning of the Age of the Thousand Year Reich and the year was that of Schickelgruber, when the world was first awakened by the cries of my humble presence. I was the third child — prematurely — in a bunch of three girls. My parents would have been regarded as working class. Being constantly plagued by illness my attendance at school suffered. I was eight years of age when I commenced regular schooling and surprisingly to me had to start at grade three.

'Adolf (Hitler) hadn't been loafing in the same manner as yours truly and was well on the way in implementing his "Lebensraum" policies. Actually I was not doing too badly myself, showing great promise of becoming a good Nazi. These traits . . . expressed themselves in my desire to wear the coveted uniform of the Hitler Youth. My father, however, wasn't having any of it once I had reached the required age and to demonstrate his opposition, accordingly, he belted merry hell out of me.'

The glamour of the uniform was replaced by fear and disillusion in the destruction of Berlin at the end of the war. But Erich survived the bombing and the Soviet occupation and completed his apprenticeship as a boilermaker in 1948. Eleven years later he emigrated to Australia where he found outlets for his enthusiasm for soccer and boxing. After a stint working at his trade in Whyalla, South Australia, he moved to the uranium-mining town of Bachelor, more colourfully known as Rum Jungle, seventy-five miles south of Darwin.

One day he found himself travelling with a workmate named Nobby in a Volkswagen Beetle from Pine Creek to Bachelor after a short holiday trip. Having driven for some time, Erich relinquished the wheel and curled up on the rear seat to sleep. When he next opened his eyes two days later he found he was in hospital and in great pain. His neck had been broken.

Apparently Erich's workmate had swerved to avoid a pothole or a kangeroo — Erich was never able to find out which because Nobby 'took off in hospital pyjamas and was never heard of since'. The Beetle left the road and turned over several times before coming to rest on its side. Nobby, who was only badly bruised in the accident, pulled the unconscious Erich out through the window and carried him a hundred yards back to the road where he had to wait for an hour before a truck came along.

After six months in the Darwin Hospital Erich was flown to Adelaide where there were better facilities but this did little for his depressed spirits. He had retained hope of recovery but in Adelaide he overheard staff discussing his condition and realized that he was now a quadriplegic for life.

'That's when I really gave up,' Erich recalls. 'I regarded my life, as I'd known it, as totally ruined. Gone were all plans for marriage and a family, and my ambition to represent my new country in an international soccer team. I became completely immersed in my misery.'

Erich was to spend two-and-a-half years in the Adelaide hospital and it was during this time he met Elizabeth Marchencko, a widow also from Germany who worked at the hospital as a nursing aide. Although considerably older than Erich a rapport developed between them and it was decided that he could escape institutionalization by building a specially designed house with his compensation money and she would nurse him there.

But life in his new home turned out to be far from idyllic. Financial pressures soon overtook them. Having to look after Erich, Elizabeth was unable to take a job while he was not entitled to welfare payment because the compensation had disqualified him through having too much in assets, meaning the house.

'There were times when body and soul threatened to part company,' Erich says. But he admits that lack of money was not the only problem, 'Having escaped the lifelong purgatory of hospital boredom, however, my own obstinacy, coupled with "the world owes me something" attitude, nearly wrecked my new found home life. Drinking became the greatest problem. How Elizabeth ever took it but remained at my side I'll never fathom and it speaks more for her than words ever will. From 1963 onwards we experienced everything except declared war, mainly due to my own inability to overcome the mounting frustrations. I just couldn't cope because whatever I undertook to find a new meaning in life was doomed to failure on account of my attitudes and disability.'

In the hope of giving him a new interest Elizabeth tried to encourage him to try painting with a mouth-held brush after reading a newspaper report on an exhibition of work by members of Association of Mouth and Foot Painting Artists. The whole idea seemed ridiculous to Erich but reluctantly he agreed to try.

He told the author, 'For no other reason but to cynically humour and deceive others to earn my daily quota of alcoholic forgetfulness, I graciously consented to mess around with paints. I can wholly endorse the benefit of having a brush handle stuck in one's mouth while suffering from a self-inflicted, blinding hangover!

'Gradually, imperceptible almost, changes occurred to soften my unforgiving bitterness towards my prevailing circumstances. Then, one day, the hitherto unthinkable occurred. There suddenly rose within me an anticipation, an unknown pleasure and a never previously known expectation of actually wanting to paint!

'There was hardly a thought about the once eagerly awaited reward after my slavery at the easel — my daily monologue with one Johnny Walker, a solitary canter on a White Horse. I discovered that there was life outside of a bottle, that there actually was another totally different world in which I could roam, an unlimited world without man-made boundaries, a limitless wonder without any restrictions and without human encumbrances of any kind. A world of the imagination — the world of painting!'

With his discovery of art, a new life began for Erich Krell. Learning to paint with a brush held in one's mouth is hard enough even without a hangover and so in Erich's own words 'I bolted the stable door of my favourite steed the White Horse and at the same time sent a long-term companion of mine Johnny Walker to take a long walk down a one-way street.'

Now his goal was to become an artist. He worked harder than he had ever worked before in his life because he felt that his survival as a person depended on success. One of his main frustrations was the fact that he could only manage to sit in his wheelchair for six hours a day, the rest of the time he had to lie prone in bed. Yet gradually his blurred attempts in oils began to evolve into landscapes based on Outback scenes which had made such a vivid impression upon him after his arrival from Europe. In 1965 his effort was rewarded by being accepted as a student by the Association of Mouth and Foot Painting Artists.

It was the first time since his Beetle had crashed on the remote road in the Northern Territory that Erich enjoyed real hope for the future. He worked as hard as ever to improve his style and changed from oil paints to the more difficult — for someone whose mobility was limited to head movement — medium of water-colour that he used in delicate paintings of native birds which he watched through his window. Each bird painting is a result of seven weeks' work.

In 1972 he attained full membership of the Association and the spectre of financial distress was exorcised.

'There was joy in the years to follow,' Erich says. 'There was sadness, setbacks, rollercoaster rides. But above all there was no mere existing, vegetating, a rotting-away in an institution. Above all there was life, there was living!'

The same year, when Erich was having a month in hospital while Elizabeth was on holiday, he met Geraldene, a new Sister in Charge, and a friendship began which later developed into something much deeper.

'Her interest and helpfulness extended gradually into my private life and she even offered to sacrifice one of her annual holidays to look after me at home during Elizabeth's next break to enable me to continue working towards an important one-man exhibition,' Erich says.

In 1977 Erich received the *Grand Prix Humanitaire de France* for 'services rendered to the Arts' and in the same year he was elected as the Australasian delegate to attend a Mouth and Foot Painters' conference in Stockholm. He flew to Europe via Bombay attended by Elizabeth and aided by a specially designed light bed frame. Before going to Stockholm Erich managed to visit Berlin where he had considered the possibility of returning but it took him less than a week to realize that a permanent homecoming was impossible.

'I seemed to be in a time warp,' he said. 'Everything appeared to have changed but, fundamentally, nothing had. People looked older, some balder — with me leading the way — but the only apparent gain manifested itself in material riches and there was tattiness and grubbiness among the ultra-modernism and glitz — it was loud, it was brash and it was ugly.'

The depression that this caused Erich was eased when he received a letter from Geraldene who wrote that she was thinking of leaving her job at the hospital to work nightshifts only and would be therefore free to look after him during the day. Such an idea was a very welcome one because Elizabeth was finding it more and more difficult to continue nursing him.

The arrangement turned out better than Erich or Geraldene expected — they married in 1978 on April Fools Day which Erich explained was 'a concession to my addled grey-matter deficiency so as not to commit the penultimate sin in forgetting our wedding anniversary!'

Since then Erich declares that they 'have lived happily ever after'. Elizabeth, now in her 80th year, resides in a self-contained flat built for her as an addition to Erich's house where he continues to paint. Writing once in the Australian *Rehabilitation Gazette* Erich said that he was not all that richly endowed with wisdom and knowledge, 'but I have learned much, even if it only gave me the opportunity to find out my own ignorance. During my more lucid moments — somewhat cynical though — I even claim that the crash which damaged my spinal cord was the best thing that could have happened to me.'

ALISON LAPPER

'I want to create a feeling.'

I did not realize I was disabled until I was thirteen — can you believe that!' declares Alison Lapper with a characteristic laugh.

To the able-bodied such a statement sounds far-fetched yet if you have grown to that age in an institution surrounded by a hundred other disabled children it is understandable. It also suggests that up until then there was no trauma because disability was the norm. The trauma came with the sudden understanding that in the world outside there were tall people with fully developed limbs who could run and dance and enjoy themselves in whatever way they wished and to whom pain was a rare annoyance easily assuaged.

'The realization came when I went to a "normal" youth club,' recalls Alison. 'It was a terrible shock. I wanted to kill myself. It was the most crucial time in my life. I had just had a major operation — they took out my ankle bone and turned my foot right round. I was starting to get interested in boys while all this was going on and I did not know what to do with myself. I felt I was going backwards rather than forward. You realize that your able-bodied friends are going to get boyfriends and you are not. It took me until I was sixteen to come to terms with my disability.'

Today she has more than come to terms with it and pursues life and a career with a zest that the able-bodied might envy but behind her easy confidence is a story of a very hard won victory.

At first sight people take Alison for a victim of thalidomide but with a flash of her quirky humour she explains, 'I'm just a natural abnormality.' She does not use the correct name for her complaint because she cannot remember how to spell it but it is phocomelia.

Alison was born in 1965 in Burton-on-Trent and as a result of phocomelia she arrived in the world without arms and legs that were no more than tiny stumps. Her mother was told with that amazing lack of tact one sometimes encounters in 'straight-from-the-shoulder-no-nonsense' medical people that if the infant survived she would never be more than a 'stuffed cabbage in a wheelchair'. It was too much for the shocked woman who left the hospital without even seeing her baby daughter.

When this limbless scrap of humanity had survived for five weeks she was taken to the Chailey Heritage, a centre for the young disabled and which was to be her home for the next seventeen years.

'Part hospital, part school, it was a little world of its own,' Alison told the author. 'At first I was in the hospital section looked after by nurses and as I grew older I progressed through different wards. I was mostly with thalidomides and there were a lot of experiments done with artificial limbs. At times we were like guinea-pigs.

'I did not see my parents until I was four and after that I stayed with them during school holidays but my real home was Chailey and it was really good for someone like me. The staff pushed you the whole time. The message was always, "You must be independent — you must do it on your own."

'Chailey was my life, and I used to think "What am I going to do when I leave here?" When the time came to go I was so petrified at the thought of leaving that I refused to budge. It took four people to put me on the coach.'

From Chailey Alison went to the Banstead Place Residential Centre in Surrey.

'At Chailey I had been considered a slow learner but at Banstead they really gave me a big kick up the backside — "Come on, pull your socks up, girl!"'

To get her integrated with the outside world the staff sent Alison down to the village to collect her own money and look after herself. Everything was new to her. Up until then she did not even know what a cheque was. And, wearing artificial legs, she was sent to a normal school nearby where by using a mouthstick she found a lot of pleasure in drawing. Her first efforts were little matchstick figures, pages and pages of them which like a comic strip played out stories running through her head — usually tragic love affairs.

At school she passed her CSE and at this time entered a contest that was to change her life. It was a school painting competition with a trip to Lourdes as the first prize. Alison, now graduated from her Lowry-like stick figures, painted a scene showing one of the Stations of the Cross. To her delighted amazement it was announced that she had won and a newspaper carried an article about the disabled girl who painted with a brush held in her mouth.

As with other artists mentioned in this book, the Association of Mouth and Foot Painting Artists picked up the story and after her work had been evaluated she was offered a studentship.

'When I was nineteen I insisted on coming up to London,' Alison explains. The Banstead Centre finally accepted her determination and found her a room in a hostel in Baron's Court. From here she attended the West London College to do an A-Level in art.

'I failed miserably,' she admits, 'but in other ways college was a success. It made me force myself to get over my fear of people. The College was massive — and rather rough — and I found everything hard because I felt there was something incredibly wrong about me. To try to look more normal I used to wear my artificial legs.'

The Mouth and Foot Painting Artists assumed more and more importance in her life and after she finished at the West London College arrangements were made for her to attend the Heatherly School of Fine Art situated off New King's Road. In order to go there from the ground floor flat she happily occupied alone in a quiet street in Hammersmith, the Association helped her to acquire a specially adapted Mini Metro in which she passed her driving test first time.

Another ambition Alison fulfilled was to learn to ride a horse. To do this she attended a riding school in Wormwood Scrubs where holding the reins in her teeth she joined able-bodied riders.

Alison has come a long way from the frightened girl who had to be forced onto the coach leaving Chailey and without doubt the key to her independence is her enthusiasm for art. Few able-bodied artists can have the same exhuberant love for their subject. Thanks to a portfolio of her work which she built up while at the Heatherly School of Fine Arts she was accepted by the Brighton Polytechnic for a degree course in art which she began in the middle of 1990. She hopes that this will lead to her being able to do art therapy with the disabled along with her painting.

Alison approaches art with the same gutsy confidence as she approaches life.

111

'When it comes to materials I have tried everything,' she says. 'I nearly poisoned myself with oils. Now I use gouache and water-colour. But I believe texture is equally important as the colours you use and I have painted on everything from calico to tissue paper to get effects I want. In fact I paint on anything that I can get hold of that has an interesting texture. Sometimes I build up the picture with Polyfilla to achieve a dimensional appearance.

'My paintings are mostly about people and how I integrate with them; how other people affect me and how I affect them and how I feel about life deep down,' she says. 'I love life classes and I love to paint beautiful bodies. You might think that its some sort of wishful thinking, that I am portraying how I think I ought to be but it's not a negative thing. It is not me saying "This is how I wish I was." This is me saying, "I look at your body and find it beautiful." I love life drawing and to capture the beauty of the human body is what I strive for all the time. I suppose I am saying "I know I am like I am but I can enjoy you as you are, and hopefully you enjoy me as I am."

'A lot of my work is experimental. I am always trying something different. I am fascinated by photography and I have taken transparencies of my work which I project back on to canvas and photograph again and so on, building up images and getting very interesting effects. I am eager to paint on glass, say six different sheets, put them together and shine light through. You see I want to create something more than you hang on the wall — I want to create a *feeling*.'

Recently Alison gave up using her artificial legs.

'I used to wear them to try and look more normal — I felt I ought to be 5' 1",' she explains. 'Then as I got older I thought, "Who am I trying to kid?" I don't need to have arms and legs if I can come across as a reasonable human being.

'I felt a great sense of achievement when I decided to do this and get about on the stumps I had. Now I have even been to nightclubs without them. And the more people who meet me as I am the more people will be comfortable with disabled persons.

'When people make a mistake and go to shake hands with me or hand me a cup of tea, it is not an embarrassment but the biggest compliment I could have above everything else because they forget I am disabled and just see me as Alison.'

BILL MOONEY

An insight into what was possible

Listening to Bill Mooney describe his childhood is like taking a journey back in time to a world of simple pleasures and innocence that we like to think we all knew once. The name of his world was West Meadows, a small town hidden away on the back roads eleven miles from Melbourne, Australia. Here he had been born on 11 February 1942.

'It was like Brigadoon in a way,' he told the author. 'It seemed somehow cut off from the outside world and was a great place for children to grow up in. Everything we enjoyed we did ourselves. We all swam in the local lake together, had our own sports team, arranged our own tennis tournaments and the kids even organized the West Meadow "Olympics" in 1956.

'In those days sport was my main interest. I played every sport I possibly could — I went on and on and on. I played it seven days a week in the summer and seven days a week in the winter, and it was my ambition to become a professional Rugby League player — and I think I could have, too.'

When he was ten years old Bill had another interest besides sport and his beloved horse, it was sculpting clay — a boyish hobby which was to return to his mind three decades later. The Mooney house was on the banks of a creek and he took dry clay from the bank to carve into models which he painted and then varnished. During this craze he filled a room with them and his mother still has some today.

Two days before his sixteenth birthday Bill decided to go swimming and, swinging into the saddle of his mare, he rode off to the nearby lake. It was a scorching day and on arriving at the water he took his horse in to cool off. He swam her to the opposite shore where he greeted a couple of the girls he knew. One was not a good swimmer and she asked him to fetch a long board which the children used to float on. Normally they did not play on this side of the lake but the board had drifted across and Bill dived in to get it.

'As I dived in I crunched my head on what later turned out to be a stack of used oil drums that a local farmer had dumped into the lake,' Bill recalls. 'No one was environmentally conscious in those days and to give the farmer the benefit of the doubt no one usually swam on that side of the lake which was three hundred yards across. With the impact I was immediately paralysed. And I thought I had drowned.'

When he floated to the surface the girls thought he was playing the fool. Laughing they splashed into the water and pushed him under — until he rolled over and they saw that there was something terribly wrong.

They lifted him on to the bank and pumped water from him, and that was when it was realized his neck was broken.

'The lifting and the artificial respiration saved my life but made me a quadriplegic,' Bill says, 'but I preferred to be a live quadriplegic rather than a dead swimmer. It took three hours for me to be taken to the Austin Hospital and when I arrived it was found I had an extremely high lesion — C3/4, with a bit of 5 on the spinal cord which is about as high as you can go without dying. In fact there was every chance I would die in the first twelve months.'

What followed was sheer horror for the boy who a few hours earlier had been riding his horse without a care in the world. Part of his head was shaved and he was given a local anaesthetic in each side of it.

'I was not happy about what was happening,' he says. 'I wanted to go out that night. Then they came at me with what seemed like a big drill and they started to bore into the side of my head. It did not hurt because bone has no feeling, but the noise in my head was dreadful. Soon there was a hole in each side of my skull into which they fitted a sort of calliper which was attached to a 25lbs weight via a pulley at the head of my bed. This was to keep my body straight.

'I was like this for eight weeks until a massive infection set in and they had to take it out. I was more or less unconscious for six weeks, which was fine for me but not my mother who was the only person allowed to see me.

'She fainted when she first saw me because I had been so healthy — suntanned, 5' 11" high and weighing around eleven stone — now I looked ghastly. Only the front of my head had been shaved and the hair at the back was still caked with mud from the lake because they were not able to move me. When I did come round it felt like there was a nest of bees in my head.'

After eight months Bill was transferred from the acute ward of the spinal unit to Ward 18 which had recently been established for the rehabilitation of patients who though remaining paralysed had regained their general health. In the bed next to Bill's was a man called Ken Slater who was to have a great influence on him and build up his confidence.

'He took me under his wing,' says Bill. 'He was the first really dominant influence on me. Before his accident he was management consultant and a top sportsman; he had played tennis for Australia, been a League footballer in Melbourne and Victoria's champion high-jumper. He used to take me to restaurants — we went in our wheelchairs — and he taught me the social graces and introduced me to art. He got me so interested in debating that I joined a debating society which won the Victoria championships a couple of times.'

When Bill had been in the Austin Hospital for a year he was bored and wanted things to do as now his fear was that he would vegetate like some of his fellow patients who did nothing but watch television. The problem was that he could not think of anything to do. It was the head occupational therapist, Anne Pennington, who persisted that he should go to her department despite his belief that there was no point in his case. When she finally persuaded him to try occupational therapy he began typing with a mouthstick, which he found comparatively easy, and after this he tried to write with a mouth-held pen — 'scribbly, awful writing' is how he described it.

Then Bill read a newspaper article about a man named Athol Thompson who was a member of the Mouth and Foot Painting Artists Association, an organization of which he had never heard.

'I was very interested in this as I saw it as a chance to be a useful person in the community,' says Bill.

Athol Thompson had lost both arms in an accident involving a power cable in Tasmania at the age of eight and later made a career as a singer as well as becoming one of the first members of the Association in Australia. When Bill contacted him he replied, 'Come and talk and see if you are interested in painting.'

Bill took up the invitation eagerly and as a result became very interested in the possibilities art offered.

'I bought a water-colour set and set to work but the paintings I did were terrible things,' he says. 'But I kept going and after a few months I went back to Athol who was very helpful, but told me that what I really needed was a teacher.'

Bill began to work seriously but he had to accept the fact that he did not have enough control of his brush. It was then that Anne Pennington suggested that he might colour old prints depicting Australian scenes.

'Why don't you tint them with water-colours for a start?' she said. 'It might help you to get control of the brush.'

The idea succeeded better than even she might have imagined.

'It was amazing,' says Bill. 'I had practised so hard without good results but here was something I could do.'

Before long Bill had about sixty old etchings that he had brought to life with delicate colour; people were eager to buy them and Anne suggested that he should hold an exhibition and then went to work to arrange it.

'She actually risked her job by going in and out of the city to set it up,' says Bill. 'She arranged with the head office of the National Bank to hold the exhibition, and then she and some of her friends came at night to mount the pictures.'

By the time the exhibition was opened by Lady Paton, wife of Sir George Paton, vice-chancellor of Melbourne University, there were a hundred of Bill's coloured etchings on display and one of the first buyers was the university library. By the end of the week every picture had been sold and Bill was left with orders for a further hundred.

'It took me six months to clear all the orders I received,' says Bill. 'The exhibition made quite a lot of money and it enabled me to buy things that I needed but I realized that it was not a long-term proposition. I could not see myself tinting forever so I went back to painting and now, having learned to control the brush with the etchings, I was much better.'

To get expert advice he went on Saturdays and Sundays to an art colony at a place called Eltham where a well-known artist Gaye Knox took him under her wing. Leading artists, such as Jim Wigley and the landscape painter Peter Glass, spent time giving him advice though sometimes he found the conflicting views of the artists could be confusing.

Thanks to his Eltham experience Bill became fascinated by the lives of the great artists and the history of painting, and since those days he has been to Europe to see the originals of his heroes such as Van Gogh, Manet, Alfred Sisley and the other great Impressionists who have given him so much pleasure and inspiration in life.

Apart from his weekends at Eltham, Bill continued to live in the hospital as, with his mother being separated and having to go to work, he had nowhere else to go where he could be looked after. In all he spent nearly five years in hospital where he painted each day. As his skill improved so did the number of people buying his pictures.

When he had proved his potential as an artist, the Association of Mouth and Foot Painting Artists invited him to become a student and a year later he met Erich Stegmann, the founder of the Association, when he came to Melbourne for an exhibition.

'This man just knocked me out,' says Bill. 'I have never met anybody before or since with his energy. You didn't really notice that he had no arms — just sleeves tucked into his pockets — he was so strong. He gave me an insight into what I could do, and I knew it was up to me to do it. After meeting him I was changed.'

The year 1963 was a landmark in Bill's life. The Association welcomed him as a full member and he got married and set up house with his wife Irene. A Scottish nurse, Irene had arrived at the Austin Hospital when Bill had been a patient there for four years, and after a courtship of a few months she agreed to become Mrs Mooney.

'It was a funny wedding,' Bill says. 'I had been ill with a chest infection and several doctors warned me to postpone it. But the director of the unit realized how important it was to us and allowed me to go. It was a wet, miserable and cold day and when I got to the reception Irene's mother was anxious about the way I looked, and gave me a brandy to help me along. I had been on antibiotics and the effect of the spirit on them was to bring me out in an instant rash — it looked as though I had the map of the world across my face.

'When people saw me they muttered, "There's something wrong with him — should be in hospital." A doctor warned me sternly "to lay off the grog", and Irene was told that we shouldn't go away to Sydney for our honeymoon. But — with me being wheeled away coughing madly — we did.

'Irene and I travelled round Victoria with me painting, and since then I have had exhibitions in most Australian states. Our first son Adam was born in 1968, the second Paul in 1969 and our daughter Wendy in 1970. I must say they have been terrific; they accepted my disability and have been so much help. It has been a joy to observe them grow and from my wheelchair to teach them sport. I love to watch Adam playing football; it reminds me of my early ambition to be a professional player. Paul has won silver medals for skiing but I have not been able to watch him as yet. Wendy I taught to ride and care for her horse, and she loves her horse just as I loved mine.

'One outdoor thing I can do which is something I really love, and that is kite-flying. I have the strings tied to a small stick which I hold in my teeth.'

It was through the Association that Bill began to enjoy overseas travel. In 1974 he was elected as a delegate to a conference in Toronto, flying via the United Kingdom so that he could visit Irene's family in Scotland, and on to Canada. He returned to Australia by way of California and Hawaii, sketching all the time.

Later he visited the Association conference which followed the death of Erich Stegmann, and then drove with Irene and a friend through France and Italy visiting galleries where he was enraptured by the works of the great European artists, especially the Impressionists.

In Italy, after a stay in Florence which Bill declares is the place where he would most love to live, the three travellers drove their dusty hired Renault to the Michelangelo Airport. He had noticed that a particular car had been following them for some time and when they pulled up in the airport carpark it screeched to a stop. Men with machine pistols leaped out and surrounded the Renault, shouting threats and demanding passports.

'They would not listen to us,' says Bill. 'Irene tried to explain who we were in French — her Italian was not up to it — but they took no notice and it was pretty uncomfortable looking down the barrel of a gun. The fact that a folded wheelchair was in the back of the car made no impression on them.

'Under cover of the pistols we were ordered out, and it was only when they saw me being *lifted* out that they calmed down and began to believe Irene. Apparently they were anti-terrorist police and they suspected that we were German terrorists.'

It was on a trip to the Phillipines that Bill came across a technique that was to give his painting a leap forward. One day he found himself in a shopping precinct where

116

a number of artists were painting, one of whom was using a palette knife.

'I watched him and was fascinated by this method of putting paint on canvas,' says Bill. 'I went back the following day and the man invited me into his tiny shop where with my wheelchair there was no room left for customers but he did not mind. I watched while he did three paintings and I was hooked on the technique. Back in Australia I tried it myself. I took a knife in my mouth and started to paint, and it worked. I was amazed at how easy it seemed. It changed the way I painted, allowing me to get effects with texture which reminded me of the time when I had been keen on clay modelling. I still have my first picture on the wall of my studio and always will because it marked such a breakthrough.

'Now that I paint with knives I am a very contented person despite the fact that I have been in a wheelchair for over thirty years. I have a terrific family and a wife without whom I would still be in hospital. Apart from painting I get a lot of satisfaction out of visiting schools where I give demonstrations and try to get across the point that the only difference between ordinary people and people in wheelchairs is that the latter have had an accident or an illness. Otherwise they are just like everyone else. We get the kids to try painting with brushes held in their mouths to give them an idea of what it is like.

'The other thing that gives me enormous satisfaction is helping fellow disabled painters towards joining the Association. A veteran from Viet Nam came and asked me if I could help him to paint. He has just applied to the Association and it gave me a great feeling when we got his paintings together.

'At the moment I am helping an eight-year-old boy and, at the other end of the scale, a man of 74. His name is Jack Freeland and he became paralysed from atypical motor neurone disease. He worked on farms all his life and never ever thought about painting — now he can't stop and paints every day of the week since the Association made him one of its students.'

Looking back on his life Bill says, 'My philosophy is a simple one. I try to do the things I can as well as I can — I try to accept the things I can't do as well as I can.'

BRUCE PEARDON

Bushland inspiration

*I*t is a warm summer evening in the Australian countryside. In an old fashioned horse-drawn cart a farmer, his wife and their small son are returning homeward from town. The little boy is so tired from the excitement of the expedition that he lies sleeping in the back of the cart with his teddy bear. When they are nearly home the cart lurches and unnoticed Teddy falls on to the dirt road.

On reaching home the farmer carries the sleeping child straight to bed and it is not until next morning that he becomes aware of his loss. Meanwhile Teddy spends the night on the road but with the sunrise various indigenous Australian animals gather to help him, a wombat, possum, emu, kangaroo and other bushland creatures...

The above is the opening scenes of a children's book told in verse entitled *Teddy's Night Lost in the Bush* and much of its delight comes from its lovingly painted illustrations depicting the bush animals. Ever since Theodore Roosevelt inspired the manufacture of teddy bears they have proved to be winners in children's fiction — one only has to think of Pooh, Paddington and Rupert! Here a teddy bear succeeds yet again, this time as the character who introduces young Australian children to their wildlife heritage though the appeal of the book has spread far beyond Australian shores, the latest country in which it is appearing being Sweden.

The book by Bruce Peardon, published by the Association for Mouth and Foot Painting Artists, follows the success of his first children's book *Charley the Chimney Sweep and Sooty* which was a Victorian Christmas story.

Bruce dedicated his teddy bear book to his son Ben 'in the fervent hope that his and future generations will have the opportunity to enjoy the unique fauna and flora of his homeland, Australia.'

Such a declaration is the key to Bruce's work. He built his house in a woodland setting and specializes in bush scenes and the enigmatic landscapes of Australia — his other favourite subject being children in amusing situations which has proved particularly popular on greetings cards produced by the Association.

Bruce was seventeen when he was involved in an accident that left him a quadriplegic. Two years earlier he had joined the Australian Navy as a junior recruit and after initial training at Perth was transferred to Flinders Naval Depot in Victoria. In October 1962 he and a friend went on leave together. The return journey to base was a long one and meant driving through the night. Bruce drove until fatigue overtook him and then his companion took the wheel while he went to sleep across the back seat. The next thing he was aware of was lying in a hospital bed, having no recollection of his friend dozing off, the car going out of control and the crash in which his spine was injured.

Things did not seem too bad for the first three weeks in hospital, then he had a relapse and with it came the realization that he would be paralysed for the rest of his life. As is seen by the stories of the artists in this book, each person has his or her way of coming to terms with disability. Bruce says that for the first quarter of an hour he was devastated when it was broken to him that he would not get the use of his limbs back, 'but after that I just concentrated on getting on with life. I was lucky that I was young and young people are adaptable.'

His adaptability was proved when in Melbourne's Austin Hospital he saw two patients hard at work painting with brushes held in their mouths. Bill Mooney and the late James Meath were members of the Association of Mouth and Foot Painting Artists.

'The way they painted inspired me to do the same,' Bruce recalls. 'I had painted for a hobby and strangely enough to paint with a brush held between my teeth — apart from the problem of biting the end off from time to time — seemed a perfectly natural way to paint right from the start. We are all part of the animal kingdom and animals have a knack of adapting very quickly to changes in their condition, and so it was for me. When I could no longer use my hands I found I could write almost immediately with a pencil held between my teeth, so when it came to painting I had no difficulty in using a brush this way. It was learning the correct techniques of painting that I had to concentrate on.'

One odd thing that he found was that being left-handed he paints with the brush held in the left side of his mouth.

For the next two years he persevered at his easel and studied the effect of colours upon each other, perspective and composition until he felt confident enough to follow the example of the other two mouth-painters and apply to the Association to become a student. His hard work was rewarded when the samples he submitted were judged to be of a high enough standard for his application to be accepted.

Soon after he was enjoying the benefits of being a student a big change took place in Bruce's life. No matter how well a severely disabled person is cared for in hospital he or she tends to become institutionalized, and Bruce and some other disabled people in the hospital wanted to prove that they could live outside hospital and by doing so it would be cheaper for the Social Services to maintain them. They acquired a house and set up their own community which, while not unique in Australia today, was a brave pioneering project in the 'sixties.

It was lack of funds which ended the experiment but it had given Bruce a taste of independence and he had no wish to go back to an institutional life. Helped by his income from the Association he managed to get a house of his own where he arranged for a young married couple to look after him in return for accommodation. Here he spent his time working to improve his painting as full membership of the Association was now his goal. He found it impossible to attend ordinary art classes so he worked on a programme of self-instruction in which he toured galleries to familiarize himself with the work of well-known artists, and studied art books to analyse the techniques of classic painters.

During this time he evolved his own philosophy of art, saying, 'I think there is too much pretentiousness in the art world — people think one has to be a Van Gogh, or starve to death in a garret. I believe one has to paint to live, and therefore I look upon myself as a commercial painter in that if I am commissioned to do a landscape or a portrait that is exactly what I have to do.'

In 1970, after Bruce had been working as a student for six years, his goal was achieved and he was made a full member of the Association, and soon afterwards held several one-man exhibitions of his work. It was a good year, but what capped it was his meeting with a nurse named Christine Halliday whom he married in 1973. Four years later they were able to buy a piece of land set in Bruce's beloved bushland seventeen miles south-west of Brisbane and here they had their house built.

'It's very conducive to painting,' says Bruce, 'being surrounded by lovely trees and plenty of animal and bird life.' The latter no doubt provided inspiration for *Teddy's Night Lost in the Bush*.

In 1983 Benjamin was born to Christine and Bruce who felt more frustration that he had ever experienced in twenty years of being disabled at not being able to pick up his son. He suffered an ache at not being able to give him a hug if he fell over or lift him on to his knee to tell him stories, but this passed with time and Benjamin learning to walk so that he could race to Bruce's wheelchair if he was in trouble. Before long he understood that his Dad could not do things like him and he began to help Bruce by fetching things for him and even helping him to adjust his easel. This seemed so natural to the boy that when he began drawing for the first time he held the pencil in his mouth.

Bruce's child studies which have proved so popular are mostly modelled on Benjamin. Boys are too lively to hold poses so his mother shoots rolls of film of him to freeze a gesture or a passing smile for Bruce to paint. For such paintings, which are used for cards, Bruce uses gouache because of its opaque colour effect, but for his landscapes he prefers to work in oils.

Sometimes it seems to Bruce there is not enough time for him to do all the things he wants to. Apart from his regular painting, he visits schools to demonstrate mouth painting as part of his talks on the subject of disability and he also takes a great — and much appreciated — interest in his fellow mouth-painting artists. With Christine he makes long journeys about the continent in order to find landscapes which she will photograph for future reference, and on several occasions they have travelled overseas together to attend international conferences arranged by the Association.

When he is not painting in his bushland home he likes to relax by watching sport — Rugby Union and cricket in particular — on television or listening to music which ranges from Aussie folk songs to Beethoven.

ERICH KRELL   *Major Mitchell Cockatoo*   Mixtechnic   40 x 27 cm

ERICH KRELL
Black Swan & Young
Mixtechnic   53 x 61 cm

ERICH KRELL
Geranium
Oil   47 x 36 cm

ERICH KRELL   *Sunset*   Oil

ERICH KRELL
Large White Heron
Oil   53 x 38 cm

123

KRIS KIRK
Stairway to Home
Oil   45 x 35 cm

KRIS KIRK
Cyprus Fishing Boat
Oil   30 x 40 cm

KRIS KIRK
Church in Cyprus
Oil 30 x 25 cm

KRIS KIRK *The Garden Bridge* Oil 36 x 46 cm

ALISON LAPPER
Leaning Figure
Watercolour   41 x 61 cm

ALISON LAPPER
Collage
Various   41 x 61 cm

ALISON LAPPER *Girl in Chair* Watercolour 61 x 85 cm

WILLIAM W. MOONEY *Boabob Tree* Oil 40 x 50 cm

WILLIAM W. MOONEY *Evening on the Sea* Watercolour 33 x 41 cm

WILLIAM W. MOONEY   *Apostles*   Oil   43 x 62 cm

WILLIAM W. MOONEY   *Hilly Scene*   Oil

BRUCE PEARDON
Childrens' World
Watercolour

BRUCE PEARDON   *Australian Bush*   Watercolour   19 x 27 cm

BRUCE PEARDON   *The Last Snow*   Watercolour   26 x 36 cm

BRUCE PEARDON *Australian Animals* Watercolour

BRUCE PEARDON
News Retriever
Watercolour   26 x 35 cm

BRUCE PEARDON   *Sick Teddy*   Watercolour

JOHN SAVAGE
Church in the Wood
Oil   35 x 25 cm

JOHN SAVAGE   *In the Grip of Winter*   Watercolour   30 x 24 cm

135

MOJGAN SAFA
Birds
Oil   42 x 54 cm

MOJGAN SAFA
Still Life
Oil   35 x 45 cm

MOJGAN SAFA

'Everything depends on one's self.'

It was an Aladdin's Cave, a gallery of treasures but not of precious stones and ingots of gold. The treasures here hung on the walls, paintings that seemed to the awe-struck girl beyond the doorway to glow as though they contained an inner light. Slowly she ventured inside, her wheelchair squeaking on the polished floor as she used her leg to haul herself forward. An art class was in progress and the noise made a number of people turn and gaze at the intruder but the man in charge smiled at her and invited her to stay.

When the class was over he spoke to the pretty girl in the wheelchair who introduced herself as Mojgan Safa and explained that her parents had just changed their home and now had an apartment in the building above the gallery. Her father worked in the Iranian Ministry of Roads and Highways and the family had been frequently on the move but now they were back in Tehran. She had been exploring the new location when she looked through the door and had been attracted by the paintings. Seeing the class in progress had given her a wonderful idea.

The gallery director listened sympathetically as she told him that while her disability meant that she could only control one leg, she was as adept at using her foot and toes as able-bodied people were at using their hands.

Would he consider teaching her to paint?

The man smiled at the eager fourteen-year-old and agreed. It would give this unfortunate something to do to pass her lonely hours he thought, not realizing then that painting was to become the most important factor in her life.

In 1968 Mojgan's mother was seven months pregnant when the car in which she was riding was involved in an accident and overturned. Although she herself was unhurt she was fearful for the child she carried and immediately had a medical examination. Doctors reassured her that no harm had been done. The confidence their words gave her did not last when Mojgan was born a month prematurely and the midwife saw that the baby appeared to be black all over.

In Iran it was customary for children to be born at home and the midwife did not have the oxygen equipment that should have been used immediately. Yet Mojgan survived and began to look more healthy. At the time no one guessed that parts of her brain had been destroyed through lack of oxygen.

Seven months later Mojgan's mother again became anxious over the baby's condition. She did not follow moving objects with her eyes and it seemed impossible for her to hold her head erect. She was taken to local doctors and when they admitted there was nothing they could do Mojgan's parents took her to specialists in England and America. Their verdict was unanimous. It was impossible to cure the brain damage she had suffered at birth.

In Iran Mojgan grew up with her mother and father. In their troubled country there were no facilities for teaching those with such disability and she had to remain at home. Though she had no control over her body it was obvious to her family that there was nothing wrong with her mentally; on the contrary she appeared to be unusually intelligent and capable of learning very quickly. She also developed remarkable control of the limb that had remained unaffected. With her toes she sewed with needles and even used scissors to cut out material. Thus she had little difficulty in learning the technique of foot painting, and visitors to her home watched in amazement when she used her foot and toes to take the cap off tubes of oil paint, gently squeeze out the required amount on to a palette and mix the required shade.

Towards the end of the 'eighties her family moved to London and took up residence in a flat in London's Queensway area, being granted a four-year visa which hopefully will lead to permanent settlement. As yet Mojgan has not learned English and when the author met her, her aunt Vida acted as interpreter.

'She is very anxious to learn English,' Vida explained, 'and I am sure she will take to it quickly. The difficulty is in arranging for her to be taught. She is getting a computer with English-Arabic programmes and we think this will be of great help. I am sure that in a year's time she will be able to talk to you direct, in fact she already understands a lot which she has picked up from television and so on.'

In 1988 an approach was made to the Mouth and Foot Painting Artists on behalf of Mojgan and she was accepted as a student in May 1989.

'It has given her a reason for living — the chance of a professional career,' says Vida. 'Her goal is to become a full member for apart from the satisfaction of artistic recognition it would make her mind easy over her future. At the moment her mother and father, who is now retired, devote themselves to looking after her but in these cases the deep anxiety is what will happen when they can no longer cope. Membership of the Association would mean that for the rest of her life she would be able to afford the necessary help to be independent.'

Hassan Movahhednia is an Iranian artist resident in Britain, and each week he visits the Safa household to help Mojgan with her painting. For this she uses a tilted table which he made for her and this stands on the floor at the right angle for her foot while she sits in her wheelchair.

'Technically she is perfect,' says Hassan. 'She can do everything including cleaning her own brushes. My role is to teach composition and the significance of colours. When I come each week we talk about the work she has done, and my main aim is to convince her of her own ability, to give her the confidence to paint in her own way. There is something — a great feeling — inside her which she is somehow frightened to express. When I see a painting by Elizabeth Twistington Higgins I see in it Elizabeth herself, it could not be the work of anyone else. The whole thing about Elizabeth is in her canvases, and that is what I want for Mojgan — to put her individuality into her canvases.'

Frequently Hasan wheels Mojgan round art exhibitions in order to study the work of different artists, learn from them and discuss what each has to say in his or her work. On the whole Mojgan likes modern representational painting, and she explains that as yet she cannot relate to abstract paintings as 'she has not yet had enough time to get to know them.'

On the subject of Mojgan's determination to become a professional artist, Hassan says, 'Inside her there is amazing strength of will.'

When Mojgan is asked where this comes from she smiles and says that some of it comes from her mother. As for religion, she believes in god but no particular sect and unlike so many of her country-folk she is not a fatalist. Her credo is summed up in her words, 'Everything depends on one's self.'

JOHN SAVAGE

'Great joy in my work.'

A fierce wind filled the sails of the galleon so that she heeled dangerously as she raced over a foaming sea. Pennants streamed from her masthead, you could almost hear the thrumming of her rigging and incongruously on her high gilded stern was the name *Floss*.

As John Savage gazed at the first picture he had painted he was unaware that it marked a turning point in his life. At that moment his satisfaction lay in the fact that he had produced something through which he could express his thanks for support received at a period when he had every reason to feel embittered. In three years he had known despair and just when it seemed that he had got on top of his problems fate had dealt him a final blow. But whatever his feelings were over this, he counted himself lucky in having caring people about him and he was eager to show his appreciation, in this case to a nurse named Floss for whom the picture had been painted.

One of a family of thirteen, John Savage was born in Birmingham. Apart from woodwork and drawing classes he did not enjoy his schooldays and from time to time played truant. On leaving school he went into an engineering factory but after fifteen months the feeling of being 'shut in' became too claustrophobic and he went into railway wagon repair which suited him much better. After two years of National Service he returned to his work, married, settled down in Salford and became the father of three children.

So far it was what might have been termed an everyday story of a Birmingham lad, then his marriage broke up and his everyday world was shattered.

His unhappiness was compounded by the problem of caring for his children and 'at his wits' end' he moved to Somerset where he and the children stayed with his sister and brother-in-law with whom he worked in his building business.

It was while he was still emotionally stunned that through his sister he met a married couple named Frank and Brenda Coffey who befriended him.

Talking about that time Brenda remembers that John was so troubled he did not want to have anything to do with women. And John swears that it was the understanding of Frank and Brenda that 'got me going again.' He frequently visited their home and helped Frank in his work as a pig farmer. Gradually his former good spirits returned.

After two years in Somerset he decided that the time had come to return to Birmingham and set up a new home for the children. One weekend he took them to stay with their grandmother and then returned to finish the last job on which he was working with his brother-in-law. Although he would miss Somerset and his good friends the thought of the new life that lay ahead filled him with elation.

Early on a wintry Monday morning in 1965 the two men set off for Gwent for their final day's work on some new bungalows. At a crossroads a car shot out in front of them, the driver lost control on the icy road and crashed into their vehicle. When John was taken from the wreck it was found that his neck was broken.

'As a result of the accident I was in hospital for nine months — four of which I was in traction — while part of the time I was in the Stoke Mandeville Hospital,' John recalls. 'When I came out I was paralysed from the neck down and the problem was to find somewhere suitable to live. Despite the fact that they already had two children to look after, my friends Frank and Brenda suggested I stay with them. They invited me to their house for a trial period to see if they could cope. They found they could and I have been part of the family ever since.'

As he adjusted to his new mode of life John who had always been active found that time hung heavy on his hands. Like others who suffered similar and unexpected paralysis, he began to use a mouthstick for turning the pages of newspapers and books and this led to him attempting to write with a mouth-held pencil. As his confidence grew he looked about for more challenging activity and decided to try sewing using Brenda's sewing machine. His first objective was to make dresses for his two daughters. First he designed them and Brenda followed his drawings as she cut out the material which he then sewed on the machine, guiding the material with his mouth.

While he was working on the dresses a Welfare officer visited him and seeing what he was doing said that she could get him work sewing pillow cases for which he would be paid £1.50 per hundred. In the 'sixties disability payments were not as generous as they are today and John was always on a financial tightrope yet he felt the effort required to sew a pillow case using his mouth was worth more than just over three-and-a-half old pence and he declined the offer. But he still needed something more than 'dressmaking' to occupy him so he tried repairing clocks!

This was not a success. Brenda was always afraid that he would swallow a spring or cogwheel but at least the attempt showed that John was gaining confidence in using his mouth in place of his hands.

'A visiting nurse used to tease me that I was idle and suggested that I took up art,' John says. 'She loaned me a couple of books on painting and brought along an artist friend who helped to set me up with what I needed. I found it very difficult at first and stuck to using a pencil. My first "work of art" was a donkey. A friend was arranging a children's party and one of the games she planned was pin-the-tail-on-the-donkey.

'One thing seemed to lead to another and next I was asked to paint a backcloth for a school nativity play. Brenda hung up a double bed sheet with weights at the bottom to keep it taut while I painted on it. I really enjoyed it and it was used year after year at the school.' Following this he painted his first 'proper' picture, the wind-driven galleon which he gave as a present to a visiting nurse.

Before his accident John had never dreamed of becoming an artist but now he spent many hours painting for his own pleasure. What was frustrating at this time was the difficulty he had with his brushes. Holding their handles in his teeth he found he was inclined to chew through them so he tried fitting the brush in pipe stems. This worked well until they were no longer available. Great ingenuity was used in trying to find the perfect holder and everything was tried from the rubber stem off an electric kettle to plastic tubes but none was satisfactory.

One day Brenda returned home in triumph with some small bamboos which she had bought at a garden shop. With a brush fitted in one end a light bamboo stick proved ideal. But just when it seemed that John was at last well-equipped for his hobby he started to feel ill.

He explained to his visiting nurse that he felt sick and terribly weak. While he was speaking she picked up one of his bamboo painting sticks.

'What do you know about these bamboo canes?' she asked. 'Did you not realize they are treated with chemicals for the garden? You have been poisoning yourself with them.'

Regretfully John gave up the bamboos and immediately his health improved. After that he noticed the mouthpiece that a disabled friend used with his POSM equipment and since then these special mouthpieces have provided him with the perfect brush-holders.

In 1972 a nurse, who was raising money for charity, asked if she could take some of his pictures to a wine-and-cheese party she was holding. They were so well received that it was decided to hold an exhibition for the cause — twenty-five of John's pictures were shown of which twenty were sold.

A local newspaper carried a report on the work of the disabled painter and an unknown person sent the cutting to the Association of Mouth and Foot Painting Artists in London. John knew nothing of this until he received a letter from the Association expressing interest in his work. He immediately sent off six of his best paintings and soon he was invited to become a student.

'The grant from the Association has transformed John's life,' Brenda says. 'It meant that he could afford a special battery-driven wheelchair which he was able to control himself so that at last he had freedom of movement. This was followed by a Renault Trafic van with special ramps so that he could take his wheelchair on board to be clamped securely in place in order to travel in comfort. None of this could have been done on his sickness benefit.'

Another advantage of being a student is that John now has his own studio built on to the house where he lives at Norton Down Green some miles outside Bath. In this light and airy room he works for hours on end at his paintings, usually starting at 10.30 a.m. and working right through until 6 p.m. or later with only a break for a cup of tea.

John paints in oils and — like the artist Edward Burra — in water-colour applied so thickly that it almost has the effect of oil paint. His favourite subjects are animals and boats.

'Cats are the most challenging,' he says. 'It is so hard to get the texture of their fur right but so rewarding when you do. I find great joy in my work, it has given me a direction in life and I am always trying to improve in the hope of being accepted as a full member. I have had a couple of my paintings chosen for Christmas cards by the Association and I find this very encouraging.

'I do not always find painting easy. Sometimes I just look at the canvas for some hours and then suddenly I get an idea and away I go and I don't want to stop. This can present a problem because I cannot feel heat or cold — and I get too involved to check the temperature. The first thing I know is that my teeth are chattering with cold and I have to go to bed with hot water bottles.'

Apart from his painting, John travels about in his Renault van to give lectures on his work and demonstrations to Women's Institutes.

'So many people have seen the Association's cards they enjoy meeting one of the artists,' he says. 'I also visit schools for the handicapped to prove to the pupils what is possible despite the severest disability.'

141

GRANT SHARMAN

'Praise the Lord.'

'It was the beginning of a rather traumatic change in my life,' says Grant Sharman when describing the accident he suffered at the age of fifteen. The only son of parents who had emigrated from England to New Zealand in the late 'fifties, he was enrolled in King's College Boys School, Auckland, in 1975. Here he found the only sport he really enjoyed playing was Rugby and though he gave his all to the game he is emphatic that he was not a reckless player.

On 6 July 1977 he was playing as a tighthead prop in an inter-house game when he was thrown out of the ruck.

'I got so carried away on this one occasion that I dived back into the ruck without thinking, my head got wedged between two players and then the ruck collapsed,' he says. 'It was as though the world had collapsed.'

Like Trevor Wells who suffered a similar accident in England, Grant had broken his neck playing the sport he loved — and like Trevor still does.

He was taken to the Middlemore Hospital which was only a mile away and here skull tongs were fitted to his head — 'Horrible things!' After nine weeks his neck was operated on, wire being put round the vertebra and bone grafted on to either side. Five weeks later he became the first patient to be admitted to the Otara Spinal Unit, Otahuhu, which was to be his home for the next decade.

'I was very shaky when I was put in a wheelchair and I was still weak when I resumed my education,' he recalls. 'I could only manage two University Entrance subjects English and physics which I studied as a pupil of the New Zealand Correspondence School the next year.'

This remarkable institution — of which the author was once a grateful pupil — was established to educate disabled children or those who lived on farms too remote to attend school, by mail and radio programmes.

When he came to take his exams he sat in front of a typewriter tapping the keys with a stick taped to his wrists and after six hours of this he was so exhausted that he swore he would never go through such an ordeal again. But the effort was worth it. He passed and the following year he took chemistry and maths. In 1980 he did courses in English and the History of Art and finally completed a paper on economics through Massey University. But while he enjoyed studying he had to face the fact he did not know what he wanted to do with his life.

Five years after his accident Grant had recovered enough strength to drive a car specially equipped for a quadriplegic. A surgeon told him that now he was mobile he should get a job. Grant took his advice and became a receptionist for two days a week at Vision Wallpapers, Papatoetoe, where he was able to drive himself to work from the unit.

'I was very nervous at first in my wheelchair,' he remembers, 'but that job was a great turning point in my life. It was tremendous to be with people in an ordinary situation and it gave me confidence to do a lot of things. Until then I felt useless but now I had a job to do and I did it. I was particularly touched when the staff arranged a 21st birthday party for me at the office.'

Meanwhile Grant had met a member of the Mouth and Foot Painting Artists' Association named Bruce Hopkins who asked him if he would like to try painting with a mouth-held brush.

'Bruce, I couldn't hold a brush in my mouth,' Grant protested.

'That's not a problem,' replied Bruce who was renowned for his confident nature. 'Just stick it in your mouth and away you go.'

Grant laughed and under Bruce's instruction attempted to paint — and was completely discouraged.

'It was a pathetic effort,' he admits. 'I just wanted to throw it away but Bruce was very persuasive and the next night I was attempting to paint again. This time there was the slightest improvement but more importantly I was enjoying it and decided to keep trying, greatly encouraged by Bruce and my mother and father.

'Later on Bruce suggested that I should submit six of my paintings to the Association of Mouth and Foot Painting Artists. This I did only to have them returned with a note saying that the paintings were not suitable for their requirements.'

Grant was so disappointed he felt he had 'been kicked in the teeth', but the rejection had the effect of making him more determined than before. He changed his style of painting and when he was satisfied that he had improved he sent off another half dozen pictures and waited nervously for the verdict.

When the reply arrived in January 1981 and was opened for him it contained wonderful news. Grant says, 'I was really proud to sign a contract as a student with the Association. It was only after I had done this that I saw the potential of art to give me my elusive independence. I had something to focus on, and I remember my father saying, "If you become a full member you will have an income guaranteed for life." And I thought, "There are not many people, able-bodied or disabled, that that can happen to." And so I worked and worked.'

Although he did try hard he did not make the progress he had hoped. As a student he was able to have tuition but the two teachers he had for periods during the next five years did not take him in the direction he felt he should go. As a result he remained mainly self-taught and he felt disappointed in the lack of success that he wanted so desperately.

Early in 1986 this changed when a professional artist named Doreen Jones, a pleasant South African lady with a halo of snow white hair, came to the spinal unit and watched Grant at work in front of his easel.

'She just watched me but made no comment,' he says. 'Then she came again and went away, but on her third visit she said, "Can I help?" Thanks to her everything began to happen. It was like being a diamond encrusted in rock and she broke away the chips. My painting changed almost immediately, becoming more detailed and professional as she taught me nearly everything I know.

'I owe Doreen a lot of credit because she showed me how to tackle subjects I thought were nearly impossible — bush scenes, ships in full detail and other complicated subjects which was great because I wanted to be a painter who could paint realistically — *I wanted people to see what I had painted come off the canvas.*

'My breakthrough came when I painted an eagle. When I had finished it appeared as though it was about to fly out of the picture. As I looked at it I felt that at last I was getting somewhere in the art world. This feeling was endorsed in late 1987 when I received a letter to say that I had been accepted as a full member of the Association of Mouth and Foot Painting Artists. I shall never forget sitting in my room by myself and re-reading that letter and realizing that I had finally achieved something.'

Bruce Hopkins, who so cheerfully introduced Grant to painting, had died in 1985 which meant that Grant was the only full member of the Association in New Zealand though there were several students some of whom were in the spinal unit. This situation gave him a sense of responsibility. In the Association's regular journal circulated to members and students around the world there was very little mention of New Zealand artists and it became Grant's priority to put his country on the map as far as disabled artists were concerned.

'We had done very little,' he admits, 'but I like to think that in the last two years we have achieved a lot. Our work has been published overseas in America and Canada, Holland, Australia and France and I feel that we are now contributing to the global MFPA.'

One of the things that caused Grant much thought when he became a professional painter was that he felt he was not a 'natural' artist and he wondered what it was that had enabled him to achieve the degree of proficiency required to become a member.

'When I had my accident my housemaster rode in the ambulance with me to hospital,' Grant says. 'After that he kept in touch and became like an elder brother. At the time religion meant little to me but because he became converted I began to take an interest in it. In 1980 I became a Christian and I do believe that had a great deal to do with my success.

'I was very impressed with a book I read by Joni Eareckson, an amazing American artist paralysed from the neck down after a diving accident who now travels the world lecturing and singing. When she signs a painting she puts the letters PTL beneath her signature — PTL standing for "Praise the Lord". And I figure that He has a big hand in the way I paint and now I put the same initials on my work.'

Apart from his painting, Grant still enjoys Rugby, watching games at Eden Park when he can. One of his most pleasurable moments was visiting the dressing-room of the home team when Auckland won the Ranfurly Shield from Canterbury — and it takes a New Zealander to appreciate the almost mystic significance of the shield.

Grant had been in the spinal unit for ten years when he became a member and as a result he was able to have a two-bedroom cottage built to his own specification at the back of his parents' house in Papakura. The doors were made wide enough for his electric wheelchair and the kitchen and bathroom were designed specially for his use. Best of all was his studio with large windows so that for the first time he was able to work in what he termed 'splendid light'. Here he enjoys the daily company of his parents, his father often coming into the studio — according to Grant — to tell him that his painting isn't coming right. And here his friend Jilly Anderson, a nurse he met in the Spinal Unit, puts out his paints for him and helps with preparations for demonstrations and exhibitions.

There is another companion who spends a great deal of time with Grant in the studio and that is his cat Tom who has often been a model and has appeared on a calendar.

Grant moved into his new home in February 1988, revelling in the pleasure of his new-found independence. But it was not long before the Otara Spinal Unit contacted him and asked if he would go back two days a week to counsel new patients.

'If you have broken your neck or your back you have a lot of questions to ask,' explains Grant. 'An able-bodied person is not so plausible as someone in a wheelchair

— when the session is over they don't get up and walk away, they wheel away.'

Like some other disabled artists in this book Grant makes a point of giving talks and demonstrations in schools and to interested organisations. In order to gain confidence he joined the Toastmasters, an international society which promotes public speaking and debating. It is an activity that he finds thoroughly enjoyable, competing successfully in debating teams and winning a couple of competitions.

'Being nervous in public was something I have overcome,' he says. 'I still had my mind and the ability to speak. I remember when I was a student giving a demonstration of mouth painting with Bruce Hopkins in Auckland and I was absolutely terrified. Last year I painted in an arcade in Queen Street — Auckland's best known thoroughfare. One moment there was no one watching me, the next there were fifty onlookers and I wasn't scared at all. I just wanted to show people how we paint, that we are not vegetables but ordinary people who can't walk.

'It is acceptance that one strives for — to be seen not as a disabled artist but as an artist fullstop. That came to fruition for me in 1989 when I entered for the Waitaki Licensing Trust Award in which I won a merit award for a painting of a tiger.

'I was pleased with that but not nearly so pleased as I was when the judge of the competition bought my tiger. Since then I have been receiving commissions and I think I am an incredibly lucky person. Of course there are times when I get a bit low, when things don't go right, but then I think about how fortunate I am and I snap out of it. To me the great thing about being an artist is that we do spread some enjoyment and give to others instead of always receiving, and we do get to leave a bit of ourselves behind when we go.'

JOHN SMITH

'If he can do it so can you.'

'I think it's true to say I was fairly good at it — riding in rodeos,' says John Smith reflectively as he sits in his wheelchair. 'I loved all horse sports as well as just riding in the bush. That was why when I left the Christian Brothers College at the age of fifteen I became a stockman. Sitting on the back of a horse was my life.'

The job of a jackeroo certainly suited John and, after gaining experience by working in the district round Mackay in Queensland, he found himself managing a cattle property for a local doctor. If the work was hard it was also healthy and until he had mumps he had never had a day off work through illness. Because he had been so fit he tended to ignore the effect caused by the mumps, and before he was fully recovered he went out on a young horse he had just broken in.

'On the afternoon of 24 September 1971 — two days before my 25th birthday — I was mustering cattle when I blacked out,' John recalls. 'I fell from the saddle and struck a lump of hard earth with the back of my head. When I opened my eyes I found I was looking up at the belly of my horse. I'd had him shod and he was bucking over me, but I could not roll out of the way. Luckily his hooves missed me and he ran off, leaving me unable to move. I knew I had a head but I didn't know where the rest of me was.'

At that time John was engaged to a local girl and their wedding was to take place in a fortnight's time. When she saw John's riderless horse gallop home she raised the alarm and a search party set out. He was finally found lying in tall grass, lifted into the back of a station wagon and driven to the Mackay Hospital where he was told that he was not expected to see the night out.

'I was still there the next morning so it was decided to fly me with a doctor and a nurse to the Princess Alexandra Hospital in Brisbane,' says John. 'I was there for ten months and those in the hospital did their best to rehabilitate me, and after much exercise I was able to move my arms up and down a little but the use of my hands never came back. When nothing more could be done for me in hospital the problem was that I had nowhere to go. There was no nursing home in Mackay and my mother would not have been able to look after a C4 quadriplegic.'

The only answer was for John to go into a nursing home in Brisbane where he naturally looked back to the freedom he had enjoyed as a stockman working under the open sky and wondered what, if anything, the future held for him.

One morning a social worker visited him and, in trying to think of something that might occupy his time, suggested he should try painting with a brush held in his mouth, to which he replied politely that he did not think it was much of an idea.

'All right,' she said. 'I'll take you on an outing.'

The outing was to the Royal Brisbane Hospital where the bewildered John was taken through the respiratory diseases unit and wheeled into a room where a man lay on a bed.

'A machine was keeping him breathing through a tube in his neck,' John recalls. 'There were medical gadgets all round him and there was never less than one nurse in the room. He could not talk or move his arms and I was told he had not been off the bed in nineteen years. All he could do was move one foot. But there was an easel at the end of the bed *and he was painting with a paint brush held in his toes.'*

John was amazed at what he saw and learned that the man on the bed was a student member of an organisation for disabled artists. Twice John went back to see him and it was through his example that the ex-stockman who had been more interested in rodeo riding than art decided to learn to paint.

'The man's name was Russell Wolf and I thought, "John, stop being sorry for yourself — if he can do it so can you." I went back to the nursing home and had a pencil put in my mouth — and found my attempts at drawing very frustrating. Then one day I drew a house and realized I could do it.'

Meanwhile John's engagement was ended because he felt he could not impose his disability on his fiancée, and he resigned himself to spending his life in the Brisbane nursing home. It was then that he became friendly with a nurse who told him she would go to Mackay with him and there help him to lead an independent life. And so, after six years, he returned to his home town to a warm welcome by relatives and friends. But the relationship did not work out and in 1976 John found himself alone once more, but at least he was able to get accommodation in a local nursing home, the St. Vincent de Paul Home for the Aged!

'The nuns and nurses were very kind to me,' John says. 'The matron even gave me an old storeroom to work in and the West Mackay Rotary Club made me an electric easel with a mechanical slide which moves the painting so that I can paint without bending my neck. The club took a great interest in me when I thought I would be in nursing homes for the rest of my life. I was made a special member, and they organized a fishing trip to raise money to get me some tutoring. Their interest continues and I have learned so much about giving from these people.'

Some ladies from the local arts society took an interest in the disabled artist and visited him in his storeroom studio. One of them had heard of the Association of Mouth and Foot Painting Artists and chose six of his best paintings which were packed up for him and sent off. John appreciated this as a kindly gesture but privately he believed he would hear nothing more on the matter.

When he did receive a letter from the Association it came as a surprise, and a delightful one at that, because he was offered a studentship. Eric Krell, a member of the Association, got in touch with John and offered him encouragement.

'He kept me going,' says John. 'There were times when I did not feel I was getting anywhere, and then I would get a letter from Eric and I would go back to work with renewed enthusiasm. His letters always seemed to come at the right time.'

At this time another factor came into John's life. He became friendly with one of the nurses at the home; a deepening relationship developed which led to his marriage with Therese in October 1981. In preparation for this John moved into his mother's house and her garage was turned into a studio.

Exactly two years after the wedding John became a full member of the Association and, as he said, it was a big day in his life because from then on he no longer needed Government assistance — he was self-supporting thanks to his art and the Association who marketed the work of its members. And as a member he was able to arrange a loan from the international office in Liechtenstein so that he and Therese could buy a block of land close enough to the beach to hear the surf.

Here they built their specially designed house with a real studio which John finds a luxury after painting in a storeroom and a garage. Here he works on his pictures of the Australian outback which, thanks to his days as a stockman, can almost bring one of the taste of dust raised by the horses and cattle. He is also well known for his studies of native birds and recently he has become interested in painting brilliant tropical fish, Mackay being the stepping off point to the Great Barrier Reef.

The house also includes a gallery for exhibiting John's paintings which is very popular with southern visitors who come to Mackay to enjoy the winter sunshine of North Queensland. John swears that it is the best place to live in all the world.

Now well established John says, 'Painting is everything to me and I treat it as a job. I like to get up and go to work like other people. Of course I have had disappointments but I can safely say that life has been good, and as a committed Christian — although I didn't used to be — I believe everything comes from God. I am lucky to have a very supportive wife and good friends. I get great pleasure out of visiting other members of the Association to see what they are doing, particularly Margaret Greig who is a great friend and who has had us to stay with her in her home in New South Wales.'

Thanks to the Association John acquired a taste of foreign travel when he and Therese flew to Madrid in 1985 for a conference of members. When he spoke to the author he was looking forward to going as one of the Australian delegates to the next international conference of Mouth and Foot Painting Artists.

HEATHER STRUDWICK

Breathless happiness

As Heather Strudwick lay in her iron lung the voice of the ward sister reached her.

'Here's Heather's dinner, nurse, if you will feed her.'

'Must I?'

'Yes, nurse. She is your special patient and I thought you got on very well. What's wrong?'

'She's always crying,' replied the nurse.

If anyone had good reason to cry it was Heather. One way or another she had lost the three things that were the most important in her life — health, husband and baby son. Yet the words of the nurse, which she was not meant to hear, shocked her.

'I was absolutely devastated when I heard this,' she says. 'I thought about it and I decided she was absolutely right. She was so kind and nice that I was burdening her with all my problems and at eighteen she could not take it — and shouldn't have to take it anyway. It was a hard lesson but a good one and when I got it sorted out in my head I realized that if I had to be fed and looked after for the rest of my life, I had to make those who looked after me laugh and not cry. So that was the turning point.'

In fact it was the first of several turning points.

Heather was born in 1933 in Gibraltar where her father was a lance corporal in the British army. When she grew up in England she trained to become an orthopaedic nurse in Oxford where she fell in love with a young man whom she married as soon as he had completed his National Service and joined the police force. They set up home in Colchester where their son Paul was born and where Heather later took a job as an industrial nurse in a factory.

Up to this point it had been a happy story, then in 1957 Heather became a victim of poliomyelitis. So badly paralysed she could not breathe, she was sent to the Rush Green Hospital in Romford, the respiratory centre for Essex, where she was placed in an iron lung. Apart from having to come to terms with the fact that she had changed overnight from being a young woman full of energy to a dangerously ill patient, she was desperately anxious over the effect her illness would have on her husband and her child then aged one year eight months.

After six weeks she was allowed to see him through a window, the risk of infection being too great to allow him to come closer. Only her head protruded from the collar of the massive machine on which she depended for life and it was heartbreaking when he failed to recognize his mummy. This made her realize the hopelessness of her situation and it was a relief when her sister-in-law Sheila offered to take care of the little boy.

At first Heather's husband visited her regularly, then the time between his visits lengthened and often he did not turn up when he had promised. And as though this uncertainty was not enough, it was found that Heather was pregnant. She was given the agonizing choice of whether or not she should be operated on. In the end she agreed that it would be best for her to have the operation and when it was all over the doctor told her that the baby was dead.

Worried by the effect the lack of visits by her husband was having on Heather, the hospital authorities contacted the police station to which he was attached. It was suggested to his superior that he should be given special leave to visit his wife who was so seriously ill.

'But he has been given leave — and cash to cover his travelling expenses,' came the surprised answer.

The truth emerged that Heather's husband had found someone else, and the 'expenses' had been used to entertain her.

The final blow came when Heather's sister-in-law wrote to her that if she was going to continue to look after little Paul she must be allowed to adopt him legally. 'We don't want to love Paul and then lose him, but if you will agree to us legally adopting him then you will make us all happy,' she said.

This letter did more than anything else to make Heather realize that she was disabled for life. She would never be able to do anything for her son and so she had to agree to him being adopted.

Heather was to remain imprisoned in the iron lung for two years, after which — like Elizabeth Twistington Higgins — she learned 'frog breathing' in which the patient uses her tongue and throat muscles to replace the paralysed diaphragm to induce air into her lungs. Although the technique was difficult to master, it meant that Heather was able to stay out of the iron lung for longer and longer periods and though the only movement of which she was capable was a limited movement of her neck she was able to sit up in a wheelchair.

Three years after she had been admitted to the Rush Green Hospital, Heather was sent to the Nuffield Orthopaedic Centre at Oxford, the hospital where she had done her training as a nurse and where she was now welcomed with great kindness by her ex-colleagues. Here it was recognized that while 'frog' breathing did give Heather limited freedom from the iron lung, it did not allow her to do anything else and she was fitted with a newly developed Thompson Pneumabelt portable respirator. Rather like an inflatable corset, it forced air in and out of the wearer's lungs by regular inflation and deflation. Freed from having to breathe consciously Heather was able to use a mouthstick to operate an electric typewriter.

When she had been a patient in the Romford hospital for five years Heather requested to be transferred to the Mylands Hospital in Colchester to be closer to her friends who were still making the journey to Romford to visit her. In Colchester one of these friends gave her a copy of the book *God's Second Door* by J.H. Roesler which told the stories of a number of disabled artists who painted by holding their brushes either in their mouths or by their toes.

Not dreaming that one day she would be included in a book on such artists herself, Heather declared that it would be impossible for her to do anything like that. But not wishing to disappoint her friend she did try and to her surprise — despite the fact that paint ran in all directions — she rather enjoyed the attempt and kept on trying. For a short time she attended evening classes in art but because everyone became more interested in her and her method of painting than the subject she found that she was not learning anything.

150

'I had to go it alone and develop my own techniques,' she explains, but as time went by she became more and more proficient and people actually began asking her for her paintings. In 1964 she contacted the Mouth and Foot Painting Artists Association which she had learned about through the book *God's Second Door* and after her work had been evaluated was given a scholarship to enable her to take her painting further.

The following year Heather fell in love. A widower named Ron Strudwick had taken on a job as hospital porter in order to be able to live in Colchester with his daughter.

Recalling what became the happiest period of her life, Heather says, 'He used to lift me out of bed and into my wheelchair. Soon he began to look in and say hello when he was passing. And at lunchtime he would bring his sandwiches and sit beside me when I was painting outside in my wheelchair. He would squeeze out fresh paint or adjust the canvas on my easel and chat to me in a most entertaining way. I soon realized that he had an intuitive understanding, but one day I felt it necessary that I should ask him why he spent so much time with me. *Was it out of pity?* That was something I had to know.'

He replied that he enjoyed her company — pity was something that had not occurred to him.

'Then he asked me to go out with him — just as if I were a normal person,' says Heather. 'It was rather nice and he took me to Felixstowe in his car for the afternoon. As we became increasingly fond of each other we decided that our friendship must either progress or be knocked rather smartly on the head so we consulted the doctor and he told Ron that I might live for two days or twenty years. Then he wished us the best of luck.'

Ron and Heather were married and moved to a bungalow of their own which, after ten years of hospital life, seemed like an impossible dream come true.

'Looking back on the way my first marriage had ended I could hardly believe how fortunate I was to experience real love after being paralysed for so long,' says Heather. 'Ron was a very special person, completely selfless and though he was older than me it made no more difference to our relationship than my disability. We just lived for each other and used to joke that we were two old fogies, but in fact we were so happy that we didn't need anything else.'

During this happy time Heather continued with her painting, trying various mediums until she found that oil paints suited her best. Full membership of the Mouth and Foot Painting Artists was the goal for which she strove.

After five years of 'the best marriage possible' Ron died and Heather was left to cope with both grief and the renewed problem of her disability. The authorities thought it would be best for her if she returned to hospital but thanks to her father coming to stay with her she managed to remain in her bungalow for a trial period of six months. The time ran out but she fought on for her independence.

When Heather needed a hip operation she was sent to St Thomas' Hospital in London which has assumed responsibility for all the respiratory cases in the country. They were few in number and it was thought best for them to be under one central authority. By a stroke of luck the hospital was running an experimental project to find out if it was less expensive to keep such patients in their own homes rather than hospitalized. The hip operation brought Heather to the notice of the medical authorities and she was included in the project which meant she would have the benefit of paid residential help.

In March 1982 she had one of the happiest days of her life when she wrote to the Social Security authorities to inform them that she no longer required assistance as she had become financially independent — she had been accepted as a member of the Association.

'It was the best letter I have ever written in my life, thanks to the Mouth and Foot Painting Artists,' she told the author emphatically. 'It is only because of the Association that I was able to buy my house and because of their continued support I have been able to add a garage, a conservatory and purchase an almost new car. As a result my life has expanded as I can travel in much more comfort.'

The other good thing to happen was a renewal of her relationship with her son, now grown up with his own business.

'My sister-in-law Sheila has been wonderful over Paul,' Heather declares. 'She has shared him with me and when he was at school she used to ring me up to read out his reports and things like that. It has been a delicate situation but I am happy to say we never fell out. Now Paul comes to visit me with his wife and their two children.'

For seventeen years Heather enjoyed the companionship of Sasha a black poodle who had been given to her by her father soon after her husband's death. Now her animal friend is an affectionate chocolate coloured poodle named Lady.

Today Heather is looked after by two young women helpers, each staying continuously with her in her bungalow for three-and-a half days each week. During the day she uses a portable respirator fitted to her wheelchair while at night she sleeps in a conventional iron lung.

'Looking back on my life I think I am awfully lucky because I have done everything — I *do* know what it's like to swim, to run, to dance and to ride,' Heather says. 'I had a normal marriage and a baby and later after I got polio I was lucky to have another very special marriage. People who are born disabled or who are disabled very young have not had the chances I have had. Some say that by being disabled later on you have more to miss but I don't see it that way. I like to feel that I know what it's like and then I have to shut the door on regrets and just carry on.'

Heather's enthusiasm for art remains as keen as ever.

'When I start painting I know roughly the colours I shall need and a helper puts them out in blobs so that I can mix them myself,' she explains. 'The difficult part is keeping the colours the same because I paint in bits and occasionally upside down as I cannot reach across the whole canvas. It takes me three weeks to a month to complete a picture, depending how quickly it dries. You can't paint on top of wet paint so usually I have three on the go at once.'

In July 1990 Heather arranged a remarkable garden party with a pig roast and buffet for a hundred-and-thirty people. It was to celebrate her thirty-third year of 'breathless happiness'!

GRANT WILLIAM SHARMAN   *Tranquil Retreat*   Oil   60 x 45 cm

GRANT WILLIAM SHARMAN   *Winter Lantern*   Oil   50 x 40 cm

JOHN SMITH   *Rider with Three Horses*   Oil 43 x 59 cm

JOHN SMITH
Holding the Mob
Oil   40 x 30 cm

JOHN SMITH
Mallee Ringnecks
Gouache   36 x 26 cm

JOHN SMITH
Rainbow Lorikets
Gouache   36 x 27 cm

HEATHER STRUDWICK   *On the Broads*   Oil   30 x 46 cm

HEATHER STRUDWICK   *Paddy Fields*   Oil   30 x 40 cm

HEATHER STRUDWICK   *Tropical Fields*   Oil

DERRICK VANDEK *Riverside* Oil 41 x 30 cm

DERRICK VANDEK   *Yacht Race*   Oil   25 x 36 cm

DERRICK VANDEK   *Sherwood Walk*   Oil   31 x 40 cm

DERRICK VANDEK
Frozen Mill Road
Oil   36 x 25 cm

DERRICK VANDEK   *Lake in Autumn*   Oil   25 x 36 cm

PETER WILLIAM VAN DER HOLST
Southern Hills
Oil   37 x 40 cm

PETER WILLIAM VAN DER HOLST
Tulips
Oil   40 x 25 cm

TOMMY WARU
Maori Style Painting
Oil   61 x 50 cm

TOMMY WARU
Tirurua River, Coromandel
Oil   45 x 61 cm

Overleaf: TREVOR WELLS
Forest Landscape
Oil   46 x 61 cm

Trevor C Wells

TREVOR WELLS
Winter Landscape
Oil   50 x 40 cm

TREVOR WELLS   *Lake Windermere, Cumbria*   Oil   46 x 56 cm

TREVOR WELLS   *Henley Bridge*   Acrylic   46 x 61 cm

TOM YENDELL
Decorating the Tree
Watercolour   50 x 38 cm

TOM YENDELL
Horse pulling Sleigh
Watercolour   25 x 35 cm

DERRICK VANDEK

Painting an old love

There is sometimes a terrible irony when it comes to disability; it is as though some malign force imposes it upon those who will suffer most through its contrast with their previous lives. So it was with Derrick Vandek. He was a professional acrobat until a fall during rehearsal condemned him to a wheelchair for the rest of his life.

As a boy in Dunfermline, Scotland, Derrick had two great loves — sport and the outdoors. From the age of seven he took up gymnastics, and, apart from performing in local boys' clubs, he was never happier than when he was wandering in the woods and camping with the Boy Scouts. Look at his paintings today and that early love of nature still shines through.

In 1955 Derrick, who had been born in the mining village of Cowden Beath twenty years earlier, was called up to do his National Service. He decided to sign on in the army for six years rather than just serve the obligatory two as it was his ambition to see the world and he thought the best way to achieve this was by becoming a regular soldier.

One day at his basic training camp he was turning somersaults to keep up his gymnastic skills when he was spotted by a physical training instructor with the result that he was included in the gymnastic team. What could have been better for a young man with his interests, and this success gave him the confidence to apply to become a P.T. instructor. After six months training at Aldershot he received his first stripe and when he later bought himself out of the army he held the rank of acting sergeant.

Derrick found that he had a particular talent for working on the parallel bars, and it was through this that he developed an acrobatic routine most of which was done poised on one arm. Before long his act was in great demand for military tattoos and garden fêtes, and in his off-duty time he began his career as a professional entertainer. The culmination of this was an appearance at London's Victoria Palace in the 'Mr Universe Show'. Following this he was offered so much work he decided to buy himself out of the army in order to become a professional acrobat.

One afternoon six months later Derrick was rehearsing on the stage of a Manchester nightclub. Part of the act consisted of balancing by means of his left arm on a table while he juggled hoops with his feet and played a harmonica with his free hand. This part of his performance ended with a somersault from the table. This afternoon he somersaulted as usual but his foot caught in the ropes of a wrestling ring which had been erected on the stage for the evening's entertainment. Derrick hit the floor and lay there.

'I realized that I must have done something to myself,' he recalls. 'It seemed as though I could not feel my body at all and there was a lot of pain in my head. And though I could speak, the words did not come out very well.'

Derrick was taken by ambulance to the Hope Hospital in Salford where a hypodermic needle provided merciful oblivion. He came round a day later to find himself in traction. His neck had been broken in the fall.

For a while Derrick clung to the hope that he would get better. When he came out of traction he was transferred to an Edinburgh hospital in order to be close to his wife and their two-year-old daughter, but after eighteen months there he had to accept the fact that he was paralysed from the chest down and he could not use his hands. As there was nothing more that could be done for him in hospital he was allowed to go home.

It was not long afterwards that doctors spoke to Derrick again, only this time it was not about his condition but his wife's — they told him that she only had a year to live. She was unaware of her illness, and Derrick managed to keep up the pretence that all was well so that she could have as long as possible without the anxiety of knowing what lay ahead. He feared that looking after him would overtax her so he made tactful arrangements to stay with his parents who had moved from Scotland to Mansfield. There he was visiting old theatrical friends backstage when he was told that he was wanted urgently on the telephone. As he was wheeled to it he had a premonition of what he was about to hear and it was right — his wife had just died.

Bereaved and paralysed, and with the responsibility of his little daughter, life could not have been more bleak but Derrick was determined to do something more with his life than sit in his wheelchair watching television from one day to the next. The problem of his little girl was solved when her grandmother in Scotland said she would bring her up.

As for his own future, Derrick decided to go into business as a theatrical agent. With the help of his younger brother Gordon he set up his agency and through contacts he had made in show business it soon began to prosper. For a while Gordon drove him about the country but as Derrick still had some movement in his arms, though not his hands, he decided to try and drive himself. For the disabled there is probably no greater sense of independence than that provided by the motor car, but in Derrick's case his muscles had atrophied through lack of use to such an extent that he was unable to turn the specially designed steering wheel. He tackled the problem with the same determination with which he had created his business. For six months he worked at revitalizing his muscles by means of exercises with weights attached to his arms. The result was that he was as able to drive as well as an able-bodied person.

By 1970 it seemed as though Derrick had repaired his life as much as was humanly possible, yet a chance encounter which involved no more than a brief conversation with a stranger was to have an unexpected effect on him. With Gordon, Derrick was holidaying in Majorca when one day sitting on the beach he heard someone say, 'Excuse me, are you a painter?'

The question took him completely by surprise and turning his head to the lady who had put it to him he replied that he wasn't, and asked why she should think he might be.

'It's just that I know someone disabled like you who paints with a brush held in his mouth. Have you ever tried painting?'

Derrick answered that while he had enjoyed drawing at school, the idea of painting since his accident had never occurred to him.

'Then you ought to try it,' the stranger said and gave him the address of the disabled artist she knew. And that, as far as Derrick was concerned, was the end of it. Yet

170

her words had sowed a seed and after a few months Derrick remembered them and the thought of painting suddenly became interesting. He wrote to the artist the stranger had mentioned and received a reply telling him about the work of the Mouth and Foot Painting Artists.

'I became so interested I decided to see if I had any ability in that direction,' Derrick says. 'And I began an oil painting of a lady in a crinoline which turned out to be the sort of painting a child might have done.'

Childish it might be, but it encouraged him to continue. When he lengthened the handles of his brushes so that his face was no longer so close to the canvas that he had to squint, his work improved despite the fact that he tended to clench the brushes so hard that on one occasion he broke his dentures. Painting reawakened his early love of the outdoors and he found that he did best with landscapes and outdoor studies, especially scenes in Sherwood Forest.

Two years after his visit to Majorca Derrick sent examples of his work to the Association of Mouth and Foot Painting Artists, the outcome of which was a letter from the Association offering a studentship.

This reply fired Derrick's ambition for, over the past months, he had come to realize how very important painting had become in his life. Being a student meant that he was able to give up his agency and concentrate solely on his art work in the hope of becoming a full-time member. This goal he achieved in 1981 — the Year of the Disabled. It was a year that will always stand out in Derrick's memory because not only did he become a professional artist in it but he met his second wife Kathleen.

At first the couple lived in a council house but on becoming a member of the Association Derrick was able to afford a mortgage on a home of their own. Today he and Kathleen spend their winters in an apartment in Spain to avoid the cold English weather which is a threat to Derrick's health.

'The flat has a big balcony on which I can sit and paint happily in the sunshine which I find very important towards keeping me fit,' he says. 'It is an ideal situation for an artist.'

PETER VAN DER HULST

Full to the brim

As a youngster Peter van der Hulst enjoyed an idyllic life. His parents arrived in New Zealand from Holland in 1957 — the year of his birth — in search of a better life. ('I think the weather here was part of the attraction,' says Peter.) They moved about the North Island before settling on their farm at the township of Ohaupo outside Hamilton. Here the family went in for dairying and fruit and pioneered the introduction of blueberries into the country.

Peter, the youngest of three brothers, loved the countryside. He also loved music and was the bass guitarist in a rock band, and he enjoyed his work as an apprentice mechanic specializing in heavy haulage and four-wheel drive vehicles. As his apprenticeship progressed it was necessary for him to take a correspondence course which meant study late into the night after working long hours during the day. It restricted his social activities and left him tired — too tired perhaps.

On the night of 21 September 1975 he was driving home from a party and went to sleep at the wheel of his car. It veered across the road, somersaulted several times and Peter was thrown out on to someone's front lawn.

'When I look back on it now it must have been a hell of a thing for my parents to be woken up in the middle of the night by a policeman saying, "Your youngest son has just had a very serious car accident — could you come to the hospital immediately,"' Peter says. On arriving at the hospital Mr and Mrs Van der Hulst were told that Peter had broken his neck and was not expected to last the night. But survive he did though for most of the next four days he was unconscious.

To this day he has no memory of the accident and has only fragmentary recollections of being in intensive care and of seeing his parents by his bed.

'But I guess my parents have always been there, and I'll never be able to say enough about how good they were,' he says. 'In the periods of time I was conscious I knew I had done something dreadful — something *bad* — to myself but no one told me what it was. I could not understand why no one would help me to get up. I did not know that I was left with a broken neck C3/4 which is pretty high. I did not know I was paralysed or in traction with skull tongs in my head and a 10lbs. lead weight stretching me out straight.'

Doctors warned Peter's parents that because of the high level of the injury he could not live very long as his breathing would not be able to cope with his condition. After Peter had been in traction for two weeks it seemed their words were justified when pneumonia set in.

'This time it was definite that I would not survive,' says Peter, 'but somehow — through the grace of God — I did.'

At that time there was no spinal unit in the North Island of New Zealand and Peter went home to spend what was expected to be a short life being cared for by his parents.

'They had no nursing experience and were helped only by a daily visit from a district nurse yet somehow they rehabilitated me,' Peter says. 'Their hard work and patience and faith in God kept me alive and gradually I started to improve until I was able to sit in a wheelchair. Then I began to wonder what was going to happen to me. I had to accept the fact that I would be paralysed from the neck down for the rest of my life and that it was a full-time job to look after me.'

During the blueberry season Peter's parents employed casual labour to pick the fruit, and some pickers came to the farm season after season. One of these was a girl who had become a good friend of the family over the years and who painted for a hobby. Seeing Peter sitting in his wheelchair without anything to occupy him she suggested that he might be able to paint with a mouth-held brush. She brought along her paints and with the help of another picker propped him up during their lunch break and watched his first attempts which later he described as 'pathetic' and made him think he was the 'least artistic person in the world.'

Despite his lack of success he found that he enjoyed putting colour on the canvas and he kept trying, helped by his friend and as ever encouraged by his mother and father. At last he got results that he felt were good enough to enter into painting competitions and to his surprise and delight he even won an award.

In 1977 the Otara Spinal Unit was opened and from time to time he was taken there for short periods in order to give his parents a rest from looking after him. Two years later he came to a big decision regarding his future and asked the medical authorities if he could stay in the spinal unit. He felt his parents had done enough for him over the past four years and now deserved to have a life of their own.

It was agreed that he should stay in the unit's long-term block and here he met Bruce Hopkins, the mouth painter, who also befriended Grant Sharman. He saw a couple of Peter's paintings and was impressed enough to suggest that he should send some samples of his work to the Association of Mouth and Foot Painting Artists which resulted in Peter being invited to become a student.

'Making that application was the best thing I ever did,' Peter declares. ' My painting suddenly had a purpose. I started to sleep better, I ate better — in fact everything was better because at last I was productive and it seemed to complement other things I was doing at the time.'

These included operating a Ham radio which enabled him to talk over the airwaves to other enthusiasts around the world, and training to be a counsellor by learning interviewing techniques at a local technical institute. Peter's counselling consisted of spending time with new patients in the spinal unit and helping them through the difficult period of readjustment.

It was while Peter was living in the unit that he met his future wife Kate though he did not know what the future held when he first saw her.

'She had applied for nursing training but had been turned down the first time so she came to Otara to do a fill-in year as a nurse-aide,' explains Peter. 'When she arrived she was the main topic of conversation among the residents and like the others living in the unit I was quite attracted to her.'

Laughing, Peter described to the author how there was a lot of competition and he wondered what chance he had of ever going out with someone like her — until he found out from friends that she was a self-confessed 'chocaholic'.

'I invited her to my room on the pretext of having some chocolate liqueur bon-bons and this gave me the chance to talk to her. Once we started talking we never stopped — and we've been talking ever since.

'Our relationship grew from that first meeting with bon-bons. Before long we discovered we were both Roman Catholics with similar Christian upbringings. This had the effect of cementing the bond between us. In the unit I went on painting and Kate continued to work in the block and we were able to see more and more of each other. It was quite a scary but exciting time for me.'

In 1980 Kate began her nursing training and in the evenings did her studying in Peter's room while he watched television with the sound turned down. One big ordeal he had to face was meeting Kate's family. She was one of six children and all were dedicated to sport which included Rugby, wrestling and netball. Peter could not help but wonder what such active people would make of him when he arrived on the scene in a wheelchair.

'I must have been a shock to them,' he says, 'but once we got to know each other there was no problem and today I could not wish for better parents-in-law. We developed a routine of visiting Kate's family for wonderful Friday-night dinners at the end of one week and going to my parents in the country the next.'

These alternating visits continued for three years until 23 April 1984 when the couple were married. They enjoyed a honeymoon in Rotorua, the town in the centre of the North Island famous for its amazing thermal springs and sulphurous atmosphere.

Some months prior to the wedding the couple had bought a house in Hamilton which was adapted with ramps to accommodate Peter's chin-controlled electric wheelchair. Here he continues to paint while Kate works part-time as a staff nurse in the Waikato Hospital. He does not feel lonely while painting thanks to the company of Solo, his eight-year-old Dalmation who lies beside his master's wheelchair while he works at his easel.

'He seems to understand that I can't pat him and he gets the message across to me that it is all right by him,' says Peter.

In 1986 the couple decided to have a change of scene. Winter had its effect on Peter's health so they rented out their house for a six-month period and flew to Hawaii, where they spent their days exploring the island in search of scenes for Peter to paint.

'It was a time out from time,' Peter says. 'And a month after our return to New Zealand we were invited to an exhibition staged by the Association in Sydney. I was so impressed by the work the Australian mouth-painting artists were showing that when I came home I realized that my work needed a shot in the arm.

'I got in touch with a professional landscape artist named Wayne Sinclair who invited me to his studio where I saw work that astonished me. He said there was no reason why I could not paint like that and it did not matter how the brush was held — all that mattered was the finished product. When I realized this I felt much better about my painting.

'Wayne not only helped me to improve my work but also to arrange annual exhibitions of it, and I shall always be grateful to him as I no longer regard myself as the least artistic person in the world. Now I seem able to see the world through an artist's eye.'

Life continues to be full to the brim for Peter. He is still a Ham radio enthusiast — 'It's great to meet people without leaving the house!' — and he still helps the newly disabled and gives talks to schools and institutions. At Christmas he enjoys family camping on the Coromandel Peninsula and other outdoor occasions which include going round golf courses in his wheelchair with golfing members of Kate's family.

Because of his love of the outdoors he and Kate have bought a section of land in the country where they plan to build a house of their own design which will include a special studio.

'I do not regard myself as an overly serious person,' Peter says, 'but I am a happy person like Kate and it's great to have a natural-smiler like her around. The main thing I have learned is that things don't happen by themselves. We need to make them happen.'

TOMMY WARU

God's returned gift

One of the most unusual pictures illustrated in the catalogue of the 1988 international exhibition of work by the Association of Mouth and Foot Painting Artists held in London's Royal Festival Hall depicted a dark, many-limbed lizard-like form against a background of Burnt Sienna surrounded by blue. This painting based on an ancient Maori motif was appropriately the work of Tommy Waru the son of a New Zealand Maori father and an Australian mother.

As a mouth-painter Tommy was encouraged to take up art by the late Bruce Hopkins who helped other disabled New Zealanders to find expression on canvas in order to relieve the tedium of their days confined to wheelchairs.

'I met Bruce in 1971 when I was in Auckland's Middlemore Hospital,' says Tommy. 'I did not find it a strain learning to use a brush held in my teeth for the simple reason that I was doing it purely for recreation — for fun. And it was really enjoyable painting with Bruce.'

Born in 1953 Tommy was fifteen when he had a diving accident that resulted in his neck being broken.

'It was totally my fault,' he says. 'I was being smart in front of some girls on a wharf. I went to dive into the sea but in doing so I tripped...'

After a year in hospital he remained paralysed from the neck down but he managed to complete his schooling and then go to university where he studied for two years before switching to technical college to become a computer programmer which he thought would give him a better chance of earning his living.

'I worked at that for three or four years,' he says. 'A lot of the time I went to work in the dark — say 6.30 in the morning — and came home equally in the dark. I finally decided that this was not for me. I wanted to see some daylight because even the windows of my office were tinted, so I left and concentrated on my painting.'

Before this Bruce Hopkins had suggested to Tommy that he should approach the Association of Mouth and Foot Painting Artists and in following this advice he submitted over twenty canvases. In August 1972 he was accepted as a student and he continued to work at his painting when not operating his computer keyboard with a mouthstick.

As Tommy's parents were unable to look after him he became a resident of the Otara Spinal Unit at Otahuhu, Auckland.

'I have been in an institutionalized environment ever since my accident,' Tommy says, 'but I decided not to become institutionalized myself which is why I get out and about so much using my electric wheelchair. Actually I am only one of many who don't want to become mothballs. I feel that a person in my position has to be occupied mentally.'

While this book was being prepared Tommy was deeply occupied in trying to save the Otara Spinal Unit from being closed due to cutbacks in hospital expenditure. He studied his old law books and attended meeting after meeting and finally had the satisfaction of learning that the unit would be saved through separate funding.

It was in the unit several years ago that Tommy's work — like that of Grant Sharman — greatly improved with the advent of the artist Doreen Jones, a South African artist who had lived in New Zealand for thirty years.

'She came on the scene in 1986 through a friend,' he says. 'She had no official connection with the unit. As a religious person she felt that we could do with some therapy as we provide therapy for the able-bodied. It is not unusual for people to bring their problems to us — and someone suicidal might go away after a long talk thinking "I'm not so badly off after all."

'Up until then my pictures had been nothing marvellous but after she began helping me their quality increased three or fourfold. She really changed my ideas of painting and yet her techniques are not imposed on us — there are four of us disabled artists connected with the unit. Indeed, if we became clones of her she would not want to teach us at all. Her aim is for us to keep our individuality and she understands one not just as a pupil but as a person condemned to staying in a chair.

'Doreen is a wonderful lady who has brought us up to the stage where we can now go ahead without her. I can't say enough about her.'

Tommy is fortunate that he has had the companionship of his girlfriend for the last fifteen years.

'The only reason we are not married is that I broke my neck before Accident Compensation came in,' he explains. 'The result is that in my case if I got married our income would be gauged jointly and all social welfare benefits would stop. I just could not afford to marry but we are hoping that this rule will be changed in the near future.'

Together they have travelled a great deal, visiting Hawaii and many Pacific islands where Tommy gained inspiration for his pictures. 'I painted in public in Hawaii which caused a lot of interest,' he says, 'and in Fiji I painted with a local disabled artist who had suffered from leprosy. He put paint on the canvas using the hair of his arms and the splotched effect was quite fascinating.'

Tommy always paints in oils because, as he says, you can come back to the painting the next day. This is important to him as he has limited endurance and painting periods are not as long as he would like.

'I like painting landscapes which are good for showing at our exhibitions of which we have a lot in New Zealand,' he says. 'There is great public interest in them especially when we go along and give demonstrations of mouth-painting.

'Of course I paint pictures which are suitable for the Association's needs and I average two pictures for the Association to one for me.'

Apart from painting Tommy, like Grant Sharman, has a burning interest in sport watching world events which are brought to New Zealand via satellite television. He also goes to watch live sport and sometimes follows Rugby teams around the country. He also finds great pleasure in his family of two brothers and two sisters.

'My elder brother is the manager of a Maori Radio station — Radio Te Roa — and my younger brother runs a hotel,' he says. 'One sister runs sauna parlours in Auckland — I used not to tell anyone that! — and my other sister is a nun. I can tell you it's great fun when we all get together.'

Although Tommy was brought up in a convent school he is not particularly religious though he does say, 'I feel that if God takes something from you — like He took my legs — He gives it back in some other way.'

177

TREVOR WELLS

Scenes you could walk into

Breezy used to be one of the most over-worked adjectives that journalists coined to describe certain buoyant characters yet this cliché word could not be bettered when applied to Trevor Wells. His characteristic expression is a happy smile and when the tape of the author's interview with him is replayed it is punctuated by gusts of laughter.

Some might think that Trevor has little to laugh about being paralysed and without feeling from the mid-chest down since he suffered an accident when he was eighteen. Yet his view of life is remarkably positive, especially since he discovered an unsuspected talent for painting.

'As far as I was concerned at school the art period was a lesson in which you did as little as possible,' he says. 'All I was really interested in was sport. I was mad about it — still am, strangely enough, though now I can only watch. When I left school I became a carpenter with a building firm and I used to play with a Rugby club in Uxbridge.'

In September 1978 he set out with his team to play a Sunday match — a 'beer match' as such games are known within the fraternity — at the grounds of the Twickenham Rugby Club.

'I did not take it seriously as I should have done,' he explains. 'It was a hot Indian summer and we were not keyed up before the game as usually happens. Indeed we put our boots on out on the pitch which you never do normally.

'There was a line out and then a scrum and in it I was too late in getting my head down. I was trapped and took the weight of the scrum on the back of my neck.'

When the scrum broke up Trevor was unable to move. An ambulance was called and he was taken to the Middlesex Hospital, and the same evening moved to Charing Cross Hospital for spinal fusion. He had broken his neck at the C4 level.

From Charing Cross Hospital Trevor was taken to Stoke Mandeville Hospital where he spent the next six months, a period of great adjustment for a young man who had lived for sport and who within seconds had been condemned to a life of immobility.

'I must confess I did a lot of heavy thinking there,' he says, 'but I like to think that I did not find it too difficult to come to terms with my disability. Of course it's hard to say so yourself but I realized that I must not have the attitude of some who felt that the whole world was against them because of an accident. I knew I had to carry on but, as I said, there were times for some pretty deep thought.'

In April 1979 Trevor was transferred to the recently opened Alderbourne Unit at Hillingdon Hospital in Uxbridge which was designed for such long-term cases and there he has lived ever since in a pleasant informal atmosphere. He has his own room and thanks to an electric wheelchair he is able to move about.

'I came here because I knew that having to cope with a quadriplegic would be too much of a burden on my mother,' he explains.

Having accepted the fact that everything had altered so drastically Trevor was able to adapt to life in the Alderbourne Unit. His interest in sport was undiminished and he certainly felt no bitterness against the game which was the cause of his accident. He watched every minute of sport that appeared on television and read newspapers, especially the sporting sections. In order to turn the pages he learned to use a mouthstick.

'And so the days flowed by just doing nothing,' he says. 'Then six years ago someone suggested that I should have a go at painting. It was something that I had never ever considered, the last thing at which I thought I would be any good. But I decided to try to pass the time and I was set up with paints and a brush fitted to my mouthstick. I must say the results at first were iffy to say the least but I became interested enough to keep going. By the time I was on my third picture I was quite amazed. I was actually painting!'

Trevor found little difficulty in manipulating his mouthstick, especially after getting one specially adapted. Remembering his Rugby days when he used a gumshield, he had an extra-light arrow shaft fitted to such a shield. The beauty of the device is that it holds the stick with a brush or pen attached perfectly steady while distributing the weight in Trevor's mouth. In this way no strain is placed on his teeth and he does not have the fatigue of having to clench them. It is so successful that his mouth-writing is better than his old handwriting.

When discussing his painting Trevor makes it sound as though it is one of the easiest things in the world.

'It is so simple — there are so few rules,' he says. 'You just have to remember that you start with the background and work forward, that light against dark throw colour up and so on.'

Such basics he worked out for himself. He never had a tutor though when he had been painting for a couple of years he tried an Adult Education course for beginners in art. This did little to help him as through hard work and experiment he was far from being a beginner.

Although the idea of becoming a professional painter did not then occur to Trevor his fascination with painting drove him on to improve his technique. He began using oil paint which he liked because 'you can move it round a bit even after a couple of days' but like other mouth-painting artists he found there were drawbacks. Brushes were difficult for him to clean and the smell of oil and turpentine gave him bad headaches. He changed over to water-colours and then found what he was looking for with acrylic paints. Although they have many of the properties of oil paints they can be mixed with water. Their main difference with oils is the dramatically shorter drying time which means the artist has to get it right within a matter of minutes.

Trevor found a direction for his art when relatives of a fellow patient at Alderbourne saw his work. By coincidence they knew the foot-painting artist Paul Driver and suggested to Trevor that he should send samples of his work to the organisation to which Paul belonged. Although he had never heard of the Association of Mouth and Foot Painting Artists he followed this advice, with the result that he was offered a studentship and within two-and-a-half years was accepted as a member.

'Through its marketing the Association makes it possible for me to earn my living with my paint brush,' Trevor says. 'I certainly could not survive on my own but by being a member of the partnership I have the benefit of its commercial outlets.'

In return Trevor concentrates on subjects which he knows are suitable for the Association to market.

'I am lucky in that what I like painting and what is commercial are combined,' he says. 'It takes me a long time to complete a picture and I can see no point in working up to four months on a painting if it is not suitable for printing.'

Four months may seem a long time even for a mouth-painter until you see Trevor's work. His outdoor scenes are made up of the most amazing detail which gives the impression that every leaf on every tree is painstakingly painted as an individual part of the whole. To achieve this his brushes are so fine that he laughingly claims that some only have a couple of hairs. The result is that his paintings have a startling clarity.

'Although I go for "printable" subjects I never paint a picture that I could not hang up on my wall,' he declares. 'I like to do scenes that you could walk into.'

And here is the clue to Trevor's success. Though he is immobile physically his inner eye roams free in the landscape he is creating. The author, who lives close to Hadrian's Wall and is used to the sight of snowy fells, could almost feel the cold emanate from one of Trevor's paintings depicting a winter scene in Cumbria.

He is particularly known for his mastery of snow in his pictures.

'I do like snow,' he agrees, 'and with the light it reflects you can get some lovely effects. Winter transforms everything and to me there is something magical about snowdrifts with the footmarks of animals printed on them, even tyre marks on a snow-covered road.'

And there is another reason why Trevor likes to do such paintings. They do not require much red paint and he has mild colour blindness when it comes to reds and greens, not that anyone could guess it when seeing an exhibition of his work.

While this book was being written Trevor was making plans to leave institutional life by moving into a home of his own. Through becoming a professional artist he has attained an independence which he could not imagine when he lay in Stoke Mandeville Hospital and pondered on what life could hold for someone who would never be able to leave his wheelchair.

'It is curious,' he muses. 'No way would I have become an artist if that accident had not happened.'

TOM YENDELL

'I even love falling down.'

When Tom Yendell begins a painting he has to decide whether to hold the brush in his teeth or his toes. One of the victims of the drug thalidomide he has the rare ability to be both a foot and mouth painting artist. He has many other talents that he uses in the service of others and this was recognized when he was chosen as one of the twelve Men of the Year in 1986.

Tom was born without arms in 1962 when his parents lived in Basingstoke. Before long the family moved to Leighton Buzzard where Tom's father had a bakery. A few years later Mr Yendell became ill with arthritis and when the Lady Hoare Trust, which was concerned with thalidomide sufferers, required someone to run its holiday home in Pevensey, East Sussex, he and his wife took the job. Here Tom went to a local primary school but as he did not appear to be doing well there he was enrolled at a prep school at the age of nine.

A year-and-a-half later he went to Treloar College at Alton in Hampshire. This establishment catering for the disabled was to have a significant influence upon his life. When Tom joined it had eighty students; today it is the biggest school for the handicapped in Britain with just under three hundred young people who are nearly all boarders. At Treloar they study an 'able-bodied' syllabus and sit for GCSEs and A-Levels.

Tom studied the 'normal subjects' for seven years at Treloar and at the end of that time decided that the only subject he was any good at was art. ('Academically I was not that bright at school,' he admits cheerfully.) He therefore went to the Hastings College of Art to do a year's foundation course in art after which he applied to Canterbury to do fine art and Brighton to do expressive art. He was accepted by both colleges and he chose Brighton Polytechnic to be near his parents who were now living in Bexhill.

At the same time he had the satisfaction of passing his driving test and owning his first specially modified car.

After two years of studying for his degree Tom was finding it hard to concentrate and felt the need to change his occupation for a while. Taking a sabbatical year he worked for the charity CRYPT — Creative Young People Together — which helped disabled youngsters with artistic talents and provided them with accommodation in bungalows around the country. Such work with fellow handicapped persons has been a theme of Tom's life ever since.

For the second half of his sabbatical year Tom went back to Treloar College. Here he worked in the art room with his old teacher who unfortunately died leaving Tom to carry on the classes until the end of the term.

Tom returned to Brighton where much of his work involved photography. He had to use a tripod to hold his camera and he found it very difficult to focus the lens. The only way he could do it was by bending down and using his feet while he looked through the viewfinder. He came up with an idea for a shoulder attachment which he designed and manufactured with John Downie an engineer from the Polytechnic. The equipment gives him mobility with his camera which he easily operates with his chin and teeth.

When he had obtained his degree Tom looked around for work and found a job with Business in the Community, an organization connected with enterprise agencies and new small businesses. He enjoyed the work but after eight months found that travelling up to London each day from his home in Lewes was a strain and he looked about for something else.

When he had been doing his foundation course in art he had contacted the Association of Mouth and Foot Painting Artists and had been told to get in touch again after he had got his degree. Now he did so and in March 1986 became a student of the Association.

Soon after this he bought an old house on the Sussex Downs with the delightful name of 'Hunter's Moon' which was in need of renovation.

'It had a great studio at the bottom of the garden,' says Tom. 'And I really enjoyed doing it up. You see I was planning to get married to a girl I had met the year before when she was doing her foundation course in art. The house was to be ready for Lucy when she finished her art degree in graphics and illustration at Bath.'

While he was having the house renovated, and painting for the Association, Tom still found time to do voluntary work for maladjusted children at the local school. It was for helping others that he was chosen as one of the Men of the Year that November which entailed travelling to London to receive his citation in company with such well known figures as Frank Bruno, Bob Monkhouse and John Mortimer.

On the eighth day of the eighth month 1988 Tom and Lucy were married — Tom saying he had chosen the date of 8.8.88 as he would easily remember his wedding anniversary. The couple went to Iceland for their honeymoon.

'Lucy was mad about Iceland,' says Tom, 'but I was rather apprehensive about going. It turned out to be a wonderful experience and now I would like to go again. We spent seven days touring the country and the rest of the time in Reykjavik. I was so impressed by the Icelandic attitude to the disabled. There they have a National Union of Disabled People which owns a specially designed building — complete with a "bank" of carers, a gym, swimming pool and craft room — where the disabled can rent apartments. Everything is run by the disabled even to having their own taxi service.'

In 1989 Tom returned to Treloar College to take up the newly created position of part-time activities co-ordinator which he thoroughly enjoys even though it meant that he and Lucy had to leave 'Hunter's Moon' in order to live in Alton. Their new house is named 'Thule' which was the ancient name for Iceland.

Being part-time the work allows Tom time to do his own painting which these days he does mostly with a mouth-held brush. When he was small he used his feet as his 'hands' but when he went as a young student to Treloar College he found that this method of working was inconvenient as the tables there were not suitable to sit on and so he changed to holding his brush or pen in his mouth.

'Although I mostly paint by mouth I can still use my foot,' he explains, 'especially when I use charcoal which does not taste very nice. I use water-colours for my painting but what I enjoy most is working in black and white. You can get such marvellous effects with black ink. I give talks and demonstrations at schools and at the

Association's last exhibition in London I had school kids sitting on the floor writing with their feet. Great fun!'

Another of Tom's ideas of fun is to go skiing in Switzerland which is the result of Lucy's encouragement. While this book was being prepared he had a holiday in Gstaad where he skied with the British Ski Team.

'I love it,' Tom declares, 'I even love falling down!'